21ST CENTURY
PRESS
PUBLISHING WITH PURPOSE
WWW.21STCENTURYPRESS.COM

Paths to Prosperity

Published by 21st Century Press

Springfield, MO 65807

21st Century Press
2131 W. Republic Rd.
PMB 41
Springfield, MO 65807

ISBN 0-9766243-8-9

Cover: Keith Locke
Book Design: Terry White

Visit our web-site at:
www.21stcenturypress.com

For childrens books visit:
www.sonshippress.com

21ST CENTURY PRESS
PUBLISHING WITH PURPOSE
WWW.21STCENTURYPRESS.COM

DEDICATION

This work is dedicated to the one through whom all things are possible, my Lord and Savior, Jesus Christ. Thank You for my countless blessings.

This book is dedicated to my mother, Geri Lee Clevenger, who through her recent illness and time in intensive care always asked about everyone else in the family. She demonstrated *agape* love and concern for those around her. I would also like to acknowledge my siblings, Cathy, Glenda and Chris who, during our mother's recent illness, showed the true meaning of family love and support.

ACKNOWLEDGEMENTS

There are those I owe a debt of gratitude and thanks, beginning with my wife, Vickie, who, in spite of putting up with me during the writing of this book, has given me continued support and spiritual encouragement. She is a guiding light for our entire family.

I would also like to thank my father Dr. CW Clevenger for always stressing the importance of good credit.

TABLE OF CONTENTS

Dear Friend:

Congratulations! You have taken the first step to prosperity. Millions of people may desire prosperity. Most will never take the steps to achieve it, and fewer will ever actualize the goal. Why? Is it flawed strategies or poor money attitudes? The purpose of this book is to empower the reader with the knowledge to attain a greater degree of financial freedom.

The book was originally divided into two sections, Credit and Financial Planning. I thought the book was complete at that point, but felt something more should be shared. People I talked with wanted to go beyond getting on the right path, they wanted a proven system of wealth accumulation. The question most often asked in my seminars was, "Would you share with us how you became successful and prosperous?"

My number one goal for this program is to get you started and set you firmly on the path to prosperity. I want to provide a whole new way of thinking and give you the tools so you can pursue your dreams. Your critical first step to becoming financially independent is to be on the right credit path to repair or improve your credit score. The second step is establishing the financial basics to put you on the right path to financial freedom.

The final section of the book focuses on a proven method of wealth accumulation that empowers you to be in control of your own financial future.

Once you have begun your path to prosperity, do not forget to give back. Throughout my life, I have witnessed the miracles of multiple returns. When I gave, it always seemed to come back. By giving back, I am not talking of money alone. Paul wrote in 1 Timothy, "The rich should be generous and share. The rich should give both money and to teach others."

So that is why I say, "Teach what you know and you shall receive more." I have found the more I teach, the more I learn. So if you want to learn more about prosperity, teach it to someone else.

> *A generous man will prosper; he who refreshes others will himself be refreshed* (Proverbs 11:25).

Again, congratulations on your first step toward your path to prosperity. I hope you will be blessed each and everyday.

May the Lord bless you.

Jerry Clevenger

PROSPERITY 101

Stay away from fools, or you won't learn a thing. Wise people have enough sense to find their way, but fools get lost (Proverbs 14:7-8 CEV).

Imagine all the good you could do if you were a little more prosperous. God wants us to continually be growing to new levels. Are you ready to expand to a greater level? Are you ready to learn some ideas that can help you have more money? When I was a college professor, I would ask students working on their MBA's why they were working so hard to earn their degree while holding a full-time job with many having families. The answer was always the same "for the money." Is the pursuit of knowledge about money? No, knowledge is about improving ones self and serving those around you. The key here is these students believed—they believed they would achieve. That is the first step, to believe you can achieve bigger and better things, and that God wants you to be prosperous so you can help others. I believe helping others improves our lives and helps you improve your own.

Prosperity in and of itself is neither good nor bad. Whether prosperity finds you generous or greedy is based entirely on *your* value system. I believe money is good for the good it can do. I know most of you have the same belief. Money is good for what it can do for you, for your family, and for so many other people and causes we care about.

MONEY: The Root of What?

Money is considered by some to carry a negative connotation. Much of this negative belief comes from misinterpreted teachings about money. The most common misconception is cited from the Bible as, "Money is the root of all evil." The actual verse is:

> "*For the love of money is a root of all kinds of evil. Some people, eager for money, have wandered from the faith and pierced themselves with* many grieves" (1 Timothy 6:10 NIV).

Is a desire for money always a root of evil? Not always. One can desire money for Christ-centered, not self-centered goals. Paul wrote Timothy to assist the young pastor with his church at Ephesus. The city was very prosperous. In fact, its tourist trade brought in so much revenue the town leaders opened the first world bank. There were many wealthy Christians that came to the church. Paul warns against the "love of money." But let's be sure we interpret his words correctly. He does not say money itself is evil (nor does any other scripture). Rather the love of money (one's attitude - something inside them, not money itself) can be a cause of trouble.

What should people with money do? Paul says they should first examine their attitudes toward their wealth. Money has a tendency to create feelings of pride, superiority, and self-sufficiency. Do not put your trust in wealth which can be easily lost, but put your faith and trust in God, the original source of wealth. In 1 Timothy 6:17-19 Paul instructs the wealthy:

> *"Command those who are rich in this present world not to be arrogant nor put their hope in wealth, which is so uncertain, but to put their hope in God, who richly provides us with everything for our enjoyment. Command them to do good, to be rich in good deeds, and to be generous and willing to share. In this way they will lay up treasure for themselves as a firm foundation for the coming age, so they may take hold of the life that is truly life."*

This I believe wholeheartedly.

What is so important about money anyway? Isn't being happy more important? The truth is Americans number one fear is running out of money. The fear has never been greater than today, as major corporations are going under leaving employees with nothing. World Com and Enron's massive fraud left thousands of people unemployed and with a total loss of retirement benefits. The love of money; the greed of a handful of individuals destroyed the financial lives of thousands.

Do not be a victim. It is about taking control of your own financial future. It is about you learning to manage money rather than letting someone else control your finances.

> *I always hear people say, "God will provide." I say, God has already provided. Go out and do something with it."*
>
> —Robert Kiyosaki
> Best Selling Author
> *Rich Dad, Poor Dad*

My pastor and I were having lunch one day with the church's finance director. I thought "what a great opportunity to discuss their thoughts on the subject of prosperity." If you think religion or politics is an exciting subject for group discussion, wait until you try prosperity and money. We had a wonderful conversation on the subject. In fact, my pastor felt we needed to look at offering some type of class to help both members and non-members in our community. This type of fellowship with others is what helps us to experience a real sense of community and encourages us to share not only our belief and thoughts, but to admit our fears and doubts.

Let's look at some of our ideas and attitudes concerning money and prosperity. Some of the questions may give you some insight into the heart of your prosperity related beliefs. Answer the following questions with whatever comes to your mind. Put down your first thoughts, do not try to edit your response.

I believe this is the place to begin a discussion of money and prosperity with others. Answer the questions on your own and then have a discussion with others, and listen to their response.

Prosperity is:

___

___

___

Wealth is:

___

___

___

___

___

Generosity is:

___

___

___

___

___

What do you remember about how your parents handled money?

___

___

___

___

___

What training or beliefs did your parents pass on to you about money and prosperity?

What were your first impressions of prosperity?

How have your views on money or prosperity changed?

If I were prosperous, I would:

If I were prosperous, I would not:

This is what I believe will happen if I become prosperous or become a more prosperous person:

If you had lots of money what would you do ?

This exercise was designed to help you gain an awareness of your beliefs about money and prosperity and to share your thoughts with others in a small group. There are so many benefits to being part of a small group dedicated to fellowship and encouragement. You may need your Pastor or someone they suggest to kick off your discussion group. I hope this exercise will take you to the next step on your path to prosperity.

DEBT MANAGEMENT

My people are destroyed from lack of knowledge (Hosea 4:6).

In 1757, Benjamin Franklin wrote, “Better to go to bed supperless, than wake up in debt.”

Today more and more Americans are going to bed stuffed–stuffed with debt. They are turning to debt to pay for lifestyles their current incomes can not support. They are determined to live better than their parents at whatever costs. Financial firms have turned credit for the masses into a huge business, aided by improved technology for analyzing credit risks. For those who are not getting a boost from workplace raises or capital gains from investments, easy credit offers a way to visually get ahead, for the time being.

The expansion of credit provides the lower and middle income earners the financial flexibility only the upper-income earners used to enjoy. Since 1990, income for the median household has risen only 11% after adjusting for inflation, while median household spending has jumped 30%, according to an analysis by Economy.com. During the same period, median household debt increased by 80%. Consumers have been on a borrowing binge. Advertisements for home equity loans are designed to tempt us to borrow more in order to have more. According to Federal Reserve reports borrowers spent half the money from refinancing their home to pay for automobiles, vacations, and other consumer luxuries.

This new advancement in credit technology has been embraced by American consumers. It seems the credit world is open 24/7. On an average week, I counted the number of credit and phone calls offering refinancing and surprisingly 10-12 solicitations were received. Calls are coming in on weekends, yes, even Sundays. Your credit and personal lives are no longer divided for many, but part of an amalgamated lifestyle that appears to have no limits.

Millions of hard-working people are failing financially. Research by the Federal Reserve indicated that household debt is at a record high relative to disposable income. Some analysts are concerned that this unprecedented level of debt might pose a risk to the financial health of American households.

More Americans filed bankruptcy last year than in the entire decade of the 1960's; each year the number of bankruptcies is at record level and is expected to increase in the coming years. It is estimated that 45 million Americans have credit problems or no credit at all.

Consumer debt is over two trillion and rising at the rate of three billion a month. Over 60 percent of all credit reports contain inaccurate, misleading, and obsolete information.

Americans are now carrying $685 billion in revolving credit card debt. According to a report by Cambridge Consumer Credit Index, 47% of the people who paid less than the full amount on their credit card bills in a recent month, made only the minimum payment due. In fact only 15% of Americans with an outstanding balance could afford to pay more than half the balance.

Over 25 years in wealth management has convinced me of one thing – most people are absolutely clueless when it comes to debt. They carry large amount of debt, and keep adding to the wrong kinds of debt. They raid their homes of equity to fuel their overspending. They reduce their retirement savings in order to spend more today. They focus on the monthly payment rather than the interest rate or term. They fail to see that their debt is growing and at the same time silently impoverishing them.

With financial hard times continuing, there will be millions of people trying to figure out how to rebuild their financial lives. And the number of people entering into this financial crisis is increasing at an overwhelming level. Many consumers who have already incurred credit problems are discovering the road from this crisis to financial recovery is very difficult.

This book offers those who have entered into credit chaos, and those on the edge, a way out. It also provides practical help by:

- Helping you manage and master your debts
- Teaching you debt negotiating techniques
- Showing you how to rebuild your credit
- Introducing you to a proven system for managing your money
- Providing you with sample letters to be used in dealing with creditors

Our financial dreams are truly at risk. The increasing threat from our overspending is leading us into credit chaos. We have wasted our efforts by following counter-productive financial strategies that have increased our frustration and our decline.

> *"Capitalism without bankruptcy is like Christianity without hell."* —Frank Borman, former CEO of bankrupt Eastern Airlines.

The volume of credit card lending nearly quadrupled between 1990 and 2000, from $173 billion to $684 billion.

Once you have acquired a bad credit rating, it is nearly impossible to avoid detection. A network of credit reporting agencies keep track of every consumer who does business or buys on credit. These agencies are the lifeblood to our credit-driven economy. Every single time you apply for credit through a bank, store, or credit card agency, or rent an apartment, or even get a phone, the prospective lender typically checks your credit with one or more of these agencies before issuing you credit.

There are over 1,800 credit reporting agencies in the United States, but there are only three large national bureaus. The top three are **Trans Union, Experian** and **Equifax.**

The reporting agencies charge a fee to businesses and creditors to obtain a copy of your credit information contained in the files. These creditors believe that the information contained in your credit file is a good indication of your creditworthiness. How you have paid other creditors in the past is an indication of how you may act in the future. They also use the credit file to verify information on your credit application.

More than likely, it is the same potential creditors who receive information about you who also provide information to the credit bureaus. When you fill out an application for credit to one of these organizations, that information is forwarded to the bureau, while constant updates on the status of your account are sent to the bureau to keep the data up to date. Not all creditors report what they know about you to the credit bureaus. And of those that do, not all report the entire contents of their files. Sometimes, the information is inaccurate and will remain on your report until you have it removed.

Lenders who deal with the credit bureaus most often for purposes of both receiving and issuing information: are the commercial banks, credit card companies, savings and loans, major department stores and finance companies. Credit bureaus add the credit information they receive from lenders to their credit profiles and sell the credit reports to creditors. A creditor that provides credit information usually receives a discount on any reports it purchases from that credit bureau.

Credit bureaus also get information from public records. Any public or court records that relate to creditworthiness are recorded. That could be divorce, tax liens, bankruptcy, judgments, or other lawsuits.

Creditors rely heavily on the information within a credit report. It is the lenders leading decision making tool. So you would assume the information would be up to date and highly accurate. This is not always the case. With billions of pieces of information being reported, errors inevitably do occur.

If your outgo exceeds your income, then your upkeep will be your downfall. Unknown

Coping With Credit Chaos

Credit chaos is the point at which you realize you can not manage your debts. You may be faced with an unexpected financial crisis as a result of illness or loss of employment. Or you could finally face the fact that years of overspending has caught up with you. Whatever the reason or cause is not the issue, but how to repair what is done or prevent any further financial decline.

Most are hoping for some quick and simple fix to their problems. The truth is that there are no simple fixes when you are in the Credit Chaos Stage.

The key to climbing out of this stage is discovery. First you discover what the current situation is, review your options, and minimize or eliminate any further damage to your financial situation. How you deal with this stage of discovery will have a major effect on both your credit and finances.

There are three steps to take once you are in the Credit Chaos Stage:

1. Discovery Phase – Pull all financial and credit records together and evaluate where you are at.

2. Know Your Options – If you don't know all your possible options, talk with someone who does. Start with a financial advisor.

3. Select a Plan of Action. The key word is action. Once you know your options, select the best plan and put it into action. Any further procrastination will only create more problems.

"Let us all be happy and live within our means, even if we have to borrow the money to do it with."
—Artemus Ward

The Theory of Pay and Pay Again Later

For most, paying off debts is a plan that will bury you in interest charges. The way some companies calculate the required minimum payments, it could take as long as 40 years to pay off your original purchase. And along the way you'll pay five times the original charge in finance charges.

It is true that buying on credit makes it possible for people, businesses, and even governments to acquire or provide things which they would not be able to do, or would have to postpone until the future, or eliminate completely. For businesses, buying on credit can be an excellent way to make money. If they invest properly, they can use the profits to pay off what they owe and have excess funds available for expansion. Many businesses could not afford to finance needed projects out of current revenues and so borrowing becomes an absolute necessity.

Because so many businesses are seasonal, the major portion of their earnings comes only at certain times of the year. They could not survive without credit to carry them during the months when revenues are lower. In theory, businesses borrow money to get through these times and then repay it when revenue flows in. Remember, businesses are taking advantage of borrowing funds that are also tax deductible, thus lowering their cost of funds. Governments do the same thing. They borrow money until tax time when they start to pull in revenue. This is only in theory. As you know, what the government borrows now our grandchildren may pay for. This is the real "Buy Now, Pay Later" plan.

Entering the wonderful world of credit can be exciting but scary at the same time. For many, buying on credit is a luxury, and for others it's an everyday occurrence. Credit gives you an incredible amount of economic freedom, but you have to be careful that you don't take that freedom for granted. Remember when you were in school and they used to tell you that anything you did, good or bad, would go on your permanent record and follow you throughout your life? Well, that's the situation with your credit. Any actions you take will have consequences that will follow you well into the future.

The "Buy Now, Pay Later" theory has encouraged many consumers to overspend. Credit cards are a way of life. Today, you can see people purchasing just about anything on credit cards. The problem with this theory is that the "pay later when my income is greater" has not materialized. Incomes have not risen to keep up with the rampant increase in debt. To make up for their inadequate incomes, debt is used to maintain their lifestyle. Instead of having larger investment portfolios, many consumers hold a large portfolio of debt that is growing quickly, with this high amount of consumer debt offering no tax deductions.

Most consumers have difficulty facing the challenge of maintaining financial stability, much less attaining a sense of financial success. U.S. households with at least one credit card owe an estimated $9,405 of debt. At a 16% interest rate they will pay $1,505 a year in interest. That is over $125 a month in interest only.

CREDIT ATTITUDE

"If a person gets his attitude toward money straight, it will help straighten out almost every other area of his life." —Billy Graham

Most of us learned what we know of credit management from our parents or by trial and error—sometimes lots of error. After years of experience, most consumers remain financially illiterate regarding the principles of credit. Most people handled their credit according to emotion or attitude. The expression, "He who dies with the most toys wins" defines the classic image of some consumers. The young consumer has more spending power than money could properly manage. Consumers today seem obsessed with spending and having. This attitude toward credit could lead to financial ruin.

Many consumers believe in two theories when it comes to debt:

1. I'll make more money later and I'll pay for it then.

2. I can always cut back on my expenses.

Typically neither of these things ever happens. You will most likely make more money "later," but your expenses have also become "more." And the idea of reducing expenses is just wishful thinking.

Let's review the credit you have had over the years and how you have managed or mismanaged it. Aside from needing this information for creditors, you should have it for yourself.

What kind of credit risk are you? You must know even more than your future creditors do. If you don't have a clear picture of how you have handled or mismanaged credit in the past, then you are likely to get yourself into trouble in the future by repeating past mistakes.

What's your attitude toward credit? You may think you know your own credit attitude without even thinking about it, since that would seem logical. The truth is most people do not. Most of us never sit down and think about our own credit attitude unless we are forced to do so and then we barely scratch the surface. We dig out the records of the past transactions we have been involved in, the car we bought and paid off, the mortgage on the house, etc., but we do not go any deeper than we have to. We look at facts and figures, but not patterns.

Credit is simply trust. When you apply for, or establish credit, you are asking someone else to trust you. They are lending you money or providing you with goods and services on the basis of your promise to pay at a later date. This principle is the same whether you borrow money from a friend or relative, charge something at a store or on a credit card, or borrow money from a bank or other lending institution. Your reputation is on the line.

Banking innovation has vastly expanded the availability of credit. Credit cards, charge accounts and installment buying, open up a whole new world of opportunity. Suddenly you can borrow in larger amounts and it is all easy and impersonal. You are not dealing with anyone you know and care about. In fact, you are probably not dealing with a person at all, just some faceless creditor. Dealing with your obligations to people is one thing, but who cares when you are just dealing with big business?

The problem with this is the big faceless creditors do not care about you either. Corporate creditors just want their money. To them, you are just a series of numbers on a balance sheet and that is all they are interested in.

That is why you should know yourself and your own tendencies before you get involved in the credit world. It is serious business. How you handle credit once you get it can affect your whole life so it deserves to be taken seriously.

> *"It is preoccupation with possession, more than anything else,that prevents men from living freely and nobly."* —Bertrand Russell

3 Stages of Your Credit Attitude

Your attitude toward credit is divided into three stages. Each stage has its own actions and creates an attitude toward credit. It has nothing to do with your age, but everything to do with how you handle your finances and your attitude, or philosophy, toward money.

Stage 1. Action - spends tomorrow's earnings today.

Attitude - Why wait? I deserve it now. Things will be better tomorrow.

This is where the majority of young couples are. They lack any real knowledge or training in personal finance. The easy access to credit leads many people to believe they must have the ability to pay or creditors will not be offering more credit. They are living life on the installment plan. This leads to financial irresponsibility and major financial problems. The unfortunate thing is it takes a long time before they realize the seriousness of the problem. Usually, the first warning sign is they are turned down for credit.

Stage 2. Action - spends today's earnings now and works at repaying debt from Stage 1.

Attitude - I have got to get out of debt. Stay out of debt. Still enjoy now.

Now facing a history of credit indulgence, they are at least aware of the problem and are concerned about what to do. Awareness is the first step in getting out of financial problems and becoming ready to take some action.

Stage 3. Action - finances tomorrow's dreams today.

Attitude - Save now. Invest as much as possible.

Unfortunately, very few ever reach this stage of credit maturity.

When examining your attitude toward credit, you want to think about where you are in these three stages. The question is:

- Is my debt increasing?
- Are my debts decreasing?
- Is my savings increasing while carrying little debt and incurring no new debt?

This book will help you no matter which stage you are in and it will provide you with the techniques to advance to the higher stage without the impact of excessive anxieties.

> *"A bank is a place where they lend you an umbrella in fair weather and ask for it back again when it begins to rain."* —Robert Frost

Creating Your Lending Profile

You must create yourself on paper if you want to get credit. You need to show lenders that you fit their statistical profile of the type of borrower they want to deal with. This is the record of all important financial transactions you have had in the last several years, how much you borrowed, and how much you have paid back. It is also the first step in deciding whether you just need to establish credit and/or build on what you already have, or whether you have to repair past damage.

Before you want anyone to know you, you want to be sure that you know yourself. This is why it is important for you to make an honest evaluation of your credit history on your own first, before you go out and start applying for credit.

You need to know what kinds of credit you are prepared to handle and what kinds might just get you in over your head. You need to honestly deal with your hidden attitudes towards money, how they developed and where they came from.

KEYS

1. Your attitudes toward credit were formed at an early age.

2. Attitudes can be improved or changed.

3. You can have almost anything. You can not have everything. You do not want it all.

If the assets outweigh the liabilities, you are okay. If it works out the other way, then you are in trouble. This may sound cold and heartless and maybe it is, but this is how lenders evaluate potential borrowers and how you should sit down and honestly evaluate yourself and your potential as a borrower.

Complete the forms on the following pages showing what you owe, to whom you owe, what the remaining balances are, what the monthly payments are, when the due date is, any payments you have missed, and any other information you think is relevant.

Once you have completed these, you can begin to get a clear picture of your situation. Then you can begin to see yourself as lenders see you. What do you look like from the lender's point of view? Are you a good risk? Would you lend yourself money if you were a lender? Let's stop for a minute and try to think about what lenders look for and how they are likely to evaluate the information they get about you.

The basic step you must take is to know your own qualifications. A lender wants to know three things:

1. Can you be trusted to repay the loan?

2. Do you have the ability to repay the loan from current earnings?

3. Do you have assets to convert to cash in order to pay the loan back?

Any loan involves first and foremost your character and trustworthiness. Can you be trusted to meet your obligations? All a lender has to go on is your track record. Have you paid your past debts in full and on time? Does he think you will do so with this loan? You must be able to convince him that you will repay the money he is about to lend you, or quite simply, he won't lend it to you.

True wealth is not a static thing. It is a living thing made out of the disposition of men to create and distribute the good things of life.

—Franklin D. Roosevelt

CREDIT SCORING

Everything should be done in a fitting and orderly way (I Corinthians 14:40).

Today, most creditors use a scoring or point system to evaluate your credit application. Items on the application are converted to points. Credit scoring is another way by which creditors determine the creditworthiness of potential borrowers. This computer-generated report is based on a statistical method, allowing creditors to make credit decisions without having to personally review loan applications. It also allows creditors to impartially evaluate larger numbers of applicants quickly and more accurately.

What is credit scoring?

Credit scoring is a system creditors use to help determine whether to give you credit.

Information about you and your credit experiences, such as your bill-paying history, the number and type of accounts you have, late payments, collection actions, outstanding debt, and the age of your accounts, is collected from your credit application and your credit report. Using a statistical program, creditors compare this information to the credit performance of consumers with similar profiles. A credit scoring system awards points for each factor that helps predict who is most likely to repay a debt. A total number of points–a credit score–helps predict how creditworthy you are, that is, how likely it is that you will repay a loan and make the payments when due.

Because your credit report is an important part of many credit scoring systems, it is very important to make sure it's accurate before you submit a credit application. To get copies of your report, contact the three major credit reporting agencies:

- Equifax: (800) 685-1111
- Experian (formerly TRW): (888) EXPERIAN (397-3742)
- Trans Union: (800) 916-8800

FICO Scores

Credit bureau scores are most often referred to as "FICO scores" because most credit bureau scores used in the United States are developed by Fair Isaac Corporation (FICO). FICO scores are provided to lenders by the three major credit reporting agencies.

FICO scores provide the best guide to future risk based solely on credit report data, i.e. the higher the score, the lower the risk. And while many lenders use FICO scores to help them make lending decisions, each lender has its own strategy, including the level of risk it finds acceptable for a given credit product. There is no single "cutoff score" used by all lenders.

FICO scores range from about 300 to 850.

Table 3

Below 640	640 – 690	690 – 780	Above 780
30%	30%	30%	10%

According to My FICO.com., July 1, 2005, the median FICO score in the U.S. stood at 723. On the same day, I had an ad on my computer to check credit scores and their lead was "the average credit score is 678." The chart above gives you an idea of average credit scores.

What a FICO Score Considers

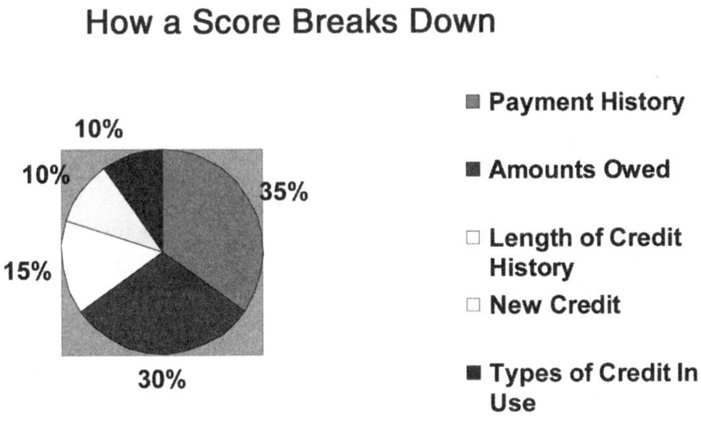

These percentages are based on the importance of the five categories for the general population. For particular groups—for example, people who have not been using credit long—the importance of these categories may be different.

1. Payment History - What is your track record?

- Approximately 35% of your score is based on this category.

The first thing any lender would want to know is whether you have paid past credit accounts on time. This is also one of the most important factors in a credit score.

Late payments are not an automatic "score-killer." An overall good credit picture can outweigh one or two instances of late credit card payments. But having no late payments in your credit report does not mean you will get a "perfect score." Some 60% - 65% of credit reports show no late payments at all. Your payment history is just one piece of information used in calculating your score.

Your score takes into account:

- Payment information on accounts
- Details on late or missed payments
- How many accounts show no late payments
- Public record and collection items - reports

such as liens, judgments, bankruptcies, foreclosures, suits, and wage attachments.

2. Amounts Owed – How much is too much?

- Approximately 30% of your score is based on this category.

Having credit accounts and owning money on them does not mean you are a high-risk borrower with a low score. However, owing a great deal of money on many accounts can indicate a person is overextended, and is more likely to make some payments late or not at all. Part of the science of scoring is determining how much is too much for a given credit profile.

Your score takes into account:

- The amount owed on all accounts

- Whether you are showing a balance on certain types of accounts

- How many accounts have balances

- How much of the total credit line is being used or credit cards and other revolving accounts.

- How much of installment loan accounts are still owed, compared to the original loan amounts.

3. Length of Credit History - How established is yours?

    - Approximately 15% of your score is based on this category.

In general, a longer credit history will increase your score. However, even consumers who have not been using credit for a long period of time may also get high scores, depending on how the rest of the credit report looks.

Your score takes into account:

- How long your credit accounts have been established.
- How long specific credit accounts have been established
- How long it has been since you used certain accounts.

4. New Credit - Are you taking on more debt?

    - Approximately 10% of your score is based on this category.

People tend to have more credit today and tend to shop for credit— via the internet and other channels—more frequently than ever. Fair Isaac scores reflect this fact. However, research shows that opening several credit accounts in a short period of time does represent greater risk - especially for people who do not have a long-established credit history. Multiple credit requests also represent greater credit risk. However, FICO scores do a good job of distinguishing between a search for many new credit accounts and rate shopping for one new account.

Your score takes into account:

- How many new accounts you have.
- How long it has been since you opened a new account.
- How many recent requests for credit you have made.
- Length of time since credit report inquiries were made by lenders.

5. Types of Credit in Use - Is it a "healthy" mix?

   - Approximately 10% of your score is based on this category.

The score will consider your mix of credit cards, retail accounts, installment loans, finance company accounts and mortgage loans. It is not necessary to have one of each, and it is not a good idea to open credit accounts you do not intend to use. The credit mix usually will not be a key factor in determining your score—but it will be more important if your credit report does not have a lot of other as "acceptable" or "unacceptable" customers. They are just one of the factors lenders use when deciding whom to loan. How big a role the score plays in the final decision depends on the individual lender.

What is a good score?

What is considered good for one lender may not be to another. Each individual lending institution decides for themselves which scores are acceptable and which are not for different types of loans or credit. The score is a number, not a recommendation. The scoring user—the lender—makes the decision. That decision may be to offer people with scores indicating higher risk, a higher interest rate rather than turning them down altogether. Or a lender might decide to lower the interest rate for someone who presents a minimal risk. It is safe to consider a score of 700 or more a strong credit score. The score of 600 or below is where most lenders put on the brakes.

How do I know my score is an accurate representation?

Scores change every time information is added to your credit file, so you do not have one single score. Your score may change when you pay a credit card bill, make a loan payment, or open a new line of credit. If you were denied credit, you should be told the reasons for the denial (called adverse notification), so you can understand your own credit risk. If you think your credit report contains mistakes which affect your credit score, you may be right. Request a copy of your credit report. An error in a credit report can affect your score. The three major U.S. bureaus—Equifax, Trans Union and Experian—all have procedures in place for correcting these errors.

Creditors establish a percentage they are comfortable with or a cutoff point. While some creditors might not consider anyone with a FICO score of 625 or less, others might thrive in that market by charging the borrower higher interest and/or greater loan fees.

Whatever their preference, the creditors can quickly and easily sort out the borrowers they want to deal with. Researching these scores, creditors have a feel for the potential borrower, at least statistically. The scores do not tell them anything about you as an individual. But once you are lumped together with a block of others with approximately the same score, the creditors have a good idea of the number of defaults there will be in a subgroup.

What the statistics really can not do is tell the creditors which subgroup you fall into. Let us say your FICO score is between 550 - 600. There is a 40% chance that you will default according to the statistics, but that does not tell the creditors whether you, as an individual, are one of the 40% who will default or one of the 60% who will not.

For example, let us say a creditor does not want anyone who scores less than 600 on the FICO score. Anyone with a rating score of less than 600 would be automatically eliminated, while those applications that scored between 600 and 650 would be referred to one of the credit examiners.

Examiners look at the human items that the statistics miss. It is their job to go beyond statistics and provide a more thorough evaluation of each applicant. For example, the evaluator would read any consumer statements attached to the credit report and weigh them into his or her final judgment. If an applicant scored low, primarily for not owning a home, or for not being on the job long enough, or for having one bad account with a creditor he had a dispute with, then the examiner may decide they are worth extending credit.

How can I improve my score?

The key to improving your score is to consistently pay bills on time. Credit scores are based on general repayment "patterns," the mix of credit cards and loans you have, and any indications that you are actively looking for more credit. Your score will improve, as you continue to handle your credit obligations responsibility. Think of a score as a "snapshot" of credit risk–it reflects your risk picture at a specific point in time. A snapshot does not change, but when another is taken, you will probably look a little different. Similarly, when your credit information changes your credit score will reflect the change. That is why lenders obtain your most recent score whenever you apply for credit.

8 Steps for Raising Your Score

1. Pay your bills on time. Delinquent payments and collections can have a major negative impact on your score.

2. Get current and stay current on all accounts.

The greater the history of paying your bills on time, the better your score.

3. Note: paying off any collection account, or closing an account on which you previously missed a payment, will not remove it from your credit report. The report will show the collection as paid. The score will still consider this information, because it reflects your past credit pattern.

4. Open new credit accounts only as needed. Do not open accounts just to have a better credit mix–it probably will not raise your score. Do not open a lot of new accounts too quickly. A new account will lower your average account age, which will have a large effect on your score if you do not have other substantial credit information.

5. Have credit cards–but manage them, having credit cards and installment loans (and making your payments) will raise your score. Those with no credit cards, for example, tend to be considered a greater risk than those who have managed their credit.

6. Keep balances low on all "revolving credit." High outstanding debt will affect your score.

7. Pay off debt and do not transfer to another account. The most effective way to improve your score in this area is by paying down your revolving

credit. In fact, owing the same amount but having fewer open accounts may lower your score.

8. Closing an account doesn't make it disappear from your report. A closed account will still show up on your credit report, and may be considered by the score. Do not close unused credit cards as a strategy to raise your score.

Other Ways to Improve or Increase Your Credit Rating:

- Apply for department store and gasoline cards. These are usually easier to get than major bank credit cards such as Visa or MasterCard.

- Consider taking out a small personal loan from your local bank or credit union and paying the money back over time. The bank may require you to put up some collateral – such as the same amount you are borrowing, deposited into a savings account. But the loan, if reported to the credit bureaus, can still help build your credit history. Make sure that it will be reported before you borrow the money.

- Apply for a secured credit card. These work something like the loan described above: You deposit a certain amount at a bank, and in return you are given a Visa or MasterCard with a credit limit equal to or greater than the amount you deposited. You can find a list of secured cards at Bankrate.com or searching online under secured bank credit card. Avoid any card that charges an upfront fee for processing your application or a high annual fee.

Once you have got credit, use it right.

- Charge a small amount on each card—but never more than you can pay off each month. You need to use credit regularly to establish your credit history, but there is usually no advantage to paying interest on those charges.

- Once you have been approved for one card or loan, do not rush out and apply for several more. Applying for too much credit will hurt, rather than help, your score. Most people need only one or two bank cards, a gasoline card and a department store card, acquired over a year or more, to start a solid credit history.

- Pay your bills on time, all the time. This includes household bills such as utilities and telephone as well as your credit card bills and loans. Late payments on any of these accounts can wind up in your credit report, and can really hurt your credit score, the three-digit number widely used by lenders to evaluate your creditworthiness.

- Do not max out your credit cards. In fact, do not even come close. Try to avoid using more than 30% or so of the credit you have available to you

—even less, if you can. Your credit score measures the difference between the credit available to you and what you are actually using. The smaller that gap, the more it hurts your score. Lenders will worry you are becoming overextended and will not be able to pay your bills if you charge too much.

How a Lower Credit Score Can Cost You

The difference in scores can have a very large effect on your costs of borrowing. Let's look at an example of exactly how much a credit score difference of 75 points can cost. For this example we will use a score of 700 and compare it to one of 625.

The difference on a monthly basis might not seem to be that great, and to most it is acceptable. However, look at it at the end of ten years. The combination of credit card and mortgage is $48,300 in interest. That is a staggering number. How many save $48,300 in ten years?

By working to improve your score, you can free up funds for investment purposes rather than wasted on high interest payments.

Credit Score	700	625
Credit Card Balance $9,000		
Credit Card Interest Rate	9.9%	18.9%
Annual Interest Rate	$891	$1,701
10 Year Difference		($8,100)
Credit Score	700	625
Mortgage $175,000		
Mortgage Rate	5.375%	8.25%
Monthly Payment	$980	$1,315
10 Year Difference		($40,200)
Life of Mortgage Difference		($120,600)

Harry to Lloyd: "I don't know about you, but I'm sick and tired of running from creditors."

—Movie: *Dumb and Dumber*

HOW TO DETERMINE IF YOU ARE IN OR NEAR CREDIT CHAOS

Warning Signs You Need Help With Your Debt

You know you need credit help when:

- Your minimum payment amounts required is a struggle to pay.
- Your credit card balances keep rising.
- You are at or near the limit on each of your credit cards.
- You do not know how much you owe, don't want to know, or are afraid of the amount.
- Receiving letters or calls from creditors.
- Using credit cards to buy necessities like food.
- Credit cards are used not for convenience, but because you do not have money.

- You are using your savings to pay monthly bills.
- Your mail reads like, "Have you forgotten us?" or "Where is our money?"
- You are minimizing on your minimum payment.
- You are so close to exceeding your maximum credit limit that every time you use your credit care, you feel like you are playing Russian Roulette. You are sure to be shot down.
- You are still charging. You do not need to cut up your credit cards; stores are doing it for you.
- You are running to the bank to deposit funds to cover checks already written.
- You have bounced checks.
- You are juggling rent or mortgage payments to pay other bills.
- Money worries are putting pressure on your relationships with others.

If any of the above scenarios sound like you, they may be more than just warning signs; you could be an official disaster candidate. Don't panic. There is a way out.

Complete the Debt Quiz located below to further determine your financial position.

DEBT 101 QUIZ

1. Do you spend more than 35 percent of your gross monthly income on rent or mortgage payments? Y N

2. Are you paying no more than the minimum on your charge cards? Y N

3. Are you unable to save money each month? Y N

4. Do you take more and more time to pay off balances on your accounts? Y N

5. Are you out of money before your next pay period? Y N

6. Do your debt payments (other than rent or mortgage) exceed 25 percent of your take-home pay? Y N

7. Are you receiving late or past due notices? Y N

8. Have you requested loan extensions? Y N

9. Does the amount of debts concern you? Y N

10. Have you used credit card advances for normal living expenses? Y N

IF YOU ANSWERED YES TO FOUR OR MORE, YOU ARE FAILING DEBT 101. BUT DON'T WORRY; YOU NEVER GET OUT OF THIS COURSE UNTIL YOU BECOME TOTALLY DEBT FREE.

Why should your report be so important to you? It not only determines the cost of borrowing, or if you are able to borrow at all, it goes much further. It also can be used in the cost of your insurance policies. One who is a greater credit risk may also be a greater insurance risk.

For many, your credit report has become the other resume. Many companies require a credit report to be part of the hiring process, thus becoming your financial resume. With the number of errors contained in credit reports, many qualified job seekers are sabotaged from the beginning. Your potential job interviewer may have already made a decision on you from the credit report and not your resume.

As president of a bank's mortgage division, I had managers come to me and tell me the story of the perfect person they wanted to hire and asked if I could make an exception in their case because their credit rating was below what the bank policy dictated. In most cases, these were talented people and would have been a great addition to our bank. However, they were too much of a credit risk. They all had good reasons for the problem, but there was nothing we could change. For most, they needed to seek employment outside of banking or any other company viewing credit reports.

What is worse, many of the people had no idea the report was that important or their rating was so low. We are talking about people with college degrees in business or finance and many with master's degrees. Your credit score is not affected if you are an MBA from a top business school or hold a GED. How can people be surprised? Get to know your report and never be surprised.

A man's treatment of money is the most decisive test of his character – how he makes it and how he spends it.

—Moffat

What Your Credit Report Says About You

The scope of the information in the reporting agencies' files can be shocking, personal, and surprisingly easy for anyone to obtain.

Credit reports are also referred to as bureau files and may vary slightly between agencies; however, most credit reports are fairly standard and outline the consumer's personal credit history.

There are four major parts to a typical credit report:

1. **Identifying Information**: Includes your full name, address and previous addresses for past years, social security number, date of birth, your present and previous employment, and your spouse's name and social security number. Length of employment and income are typically not reported, but watch the former if it is reported, because it often is incorrect. Creditors will sometimes reject an application because they "can't confirm employment." If you are self-employed, credit bureaus may have you listed as unemployed, which should be corrected immediately.

2. **Credit Information**: Lists name of issuer for the credit account, date account was opened, original balance or limit, current balance (beginning

with the reporting date, which is also listed), terms of account, and the current status of the account. The status of each item is indicated by a complicated code system that signifies exactly what has happened to the account. This leaves little room for guessing. It also leaves little room for paying a delinquent account and therefore changing the status.

3. **Public Record Information:** Includes bankruptcies, tax liens, judgments and other filings. This information is collected manually by companies or individuals whose business is researching this information to resell to interested parties. Few courts send public record information to credit bureaus.

4. **Inquiries:** Each time a creditor requests a copy of your report, it is recorded in your report and it stays on your record for up to one year. This addition is "non-evaluated" by the bureau, but it can be seen as negative if you have several inquiries with no subsequent accounts opened. Creditors who later see this will assume you were turned down even though there are other possible explanations for the inquiries.

Credit Report

In viewing a credit report, you will find the Creditor, Date Credit Opened, High Credit, Balance, Past Due Amount, Terms, Historical Statue, and Current Rating.

The key area to look at is the Current Rating. The current manner of payment is ranked as follows:

00 Too new to rate, or no rating

01 Pays within 30 days of payment due date

02 Pays in more than 30 days from the payment due date, but not more than 60 days, or not more than two payments past due

03 Pays in more than 60 days from the payment due date, but not more than 90 days, or three payments past due

04 Pays in more than 90 days from the payment due date, but not more than 120 days or four payments past due

05 Pays in more than 120 days from payment due date or more than four payments past due

06 No rating exists

07 Making regular payments under "Wage Earner Plan" or similar arrangement

08 Repossession

09 Bad debt, placed for collection

Type of Account:

R	Revolving
I	Installment
M	Mortgage
IO	Installment Loan with no payments yet

Get a Free Copy of Your Credit Report

The first step is to get a copy of your current credit report. By law, you are entitled to receive a free copy of the report if you have been denied credit within the past 30 days. Within the credit denial letter is the name of the credit bureau from which the lender acquired the information to base their decision on. In your letter to that credit bureau, include a copy of your denial letter from the creditor. Receiving a copy of your credit report, and reviewing it before applying for credit, is a very wise move. It can save you time, aggravation, and is the beginning step to repairing your credit.

Up until 2005, you had to pay $10 or more to get a copy of your credit report. Now, you can request one free credit report each year from each of the three major credit reporting agencies. It not only encourages consumers to check their credit histories, which include balances on their credit cards, autos and house payments. It also allows them to check whether or not the information is accurate.

Reviewing your credit reports on a regular basis can help you spot not only inaccuracies that could hurt your credit rating, but also fraudulent attempts by identity thieves to steal your credit.

Identity theft and potential errors were the top reasons Congress, in 2003, passed the Fair and Accurate Credit Transactions Act, allowing free reports once every 12 months from each of the three national credit reporting agencies: Equifax, Experian and TransUnion.

Consumers can get their reports in one of three ways. The fastest is to use the official Website. You can also order reports by mail. Now you can get a free credit report to make sure it offers a fair picture of your credit history.

Experts say the new law offers an unprecedented opportunity to consumers to monitor the accuracy of their credit histories. But how consumers monitor their reports depends on their individual needs. Consumer Federation of America suggests consumers string out their requests for free credit reports over the entire year. Checking their reports every four months can allow consumers to react more quickly to identity theft.

Credit reports are just the first step in monitoring a consumer's credit. The free report does not include a credit score. To receive your score you must pay one of the three big reporting agencies or obtain it from the company that developed the scoring system—FICO—Fair Isaac at www.myfico.com or go to www.annualcreditreport.com.

What Should I Look for When I Get It?

1. Your name, address, birth date, social security number and other information are correct.

2. The status and number of open credit accounts,

such as mortgages, loans and credit card balances, are correctly listed.

3. All your accounts are in good standing, are listed and accurate, whichhelp your credit rating.

4. Whether it lists credit card accounts you no longer use, which can hurt your credit rating.

5. Whether it lists any accounts you don't recognize, which can signal an error or potential identity theft.

6. What and how many businesses have inquired about your credit history within the past year.

7. Whether public information about you, such as bankruptcies, are listed correctly.

What Can I Do if I Find Inaccuracies or Errors?

1. Notify the credit reporting agencies in writing to dispute the information and include supporting material.

2. Notify the business or creditor that submitted the disputed information.

3. Send your notification by certified mail and keep a copy.

4. The credit reporting agencies must investigate the disputed items, usually within 30 days, unless it considers the dispute frivolous.

5. If the information is inaccurate, the provider of the information must notify all credit reporting agencies so they can correct your file.

6. When the investigation is completed, the credit reporting agencies must give you the written results.

For more information on your rights, go to:

www.ftc.gov/bcp/conline/pubs/credit/freereports.htm

www.annualcreditreport.com/cre/helpfaq

WARNING

If you apply for credit before reviewing your credit report, you may run the risk of having your credit application denied by the lender and this will be listed in the "inquiry" section of your credit report. Numerous inquiries on your credit report is a big "negative" to lenders, especially if the prospective lender inquires into your credit history and then denies credit because of excessive inquiries. Note: you are entitled to dispute inquiries listed on your credit report if you did not authorize them.

Your credit report from one credit reporting agency may differ from another. Because of this fact, and since you do not know which credit reporting agency your prospective creditor will utilize, you should obtain a copy from each.

Some financial advisors suggest you periodically review your credit report for inaccuracies or omissions. This could be especially important if you are considering making a major purchase, such as buying a home. Checking in advance on the accuracy of information in your credit file could speed the credit-granting process.

If you simply want a copy of your report, call the CRA's listed in the Yellow Pages under "credit" or "credit rating and reporting." Call each credit bureau listed since more than one agency may have a file on you, some with different information. The three major national credit bureaus are:

- Equifax P.O. Box 740241, Atlanta, GA 30374-0241 (800) 685-1111

- Experian (formerly TRW) P.O. Box 2022, Allen, TX 75013, (888) EXPERIAN (397-3742)

- Trans Union P.O. Box 1000, Chester, PA 19022; (800) 916-8800

Local offices can be found in most large cities, or call the above credit bureaus to obtain the address of the credit bureau nearest you.

Contact your local credit bureau in writing requesting a copy of your credit report. Include you and your spouse's name, current and previous addresses, social security numbers, and date of birth.

WHAT TO DO IF DENIED CREDIT

The rich rule over the poor, and the borrower is a servant to the lender (Proverbs 22: 17).

12 Common Reasons for Refused Credit

When prospective lenders inquire about your credit standing, they examine your record with certain expectations. To evaluate your own report, you need to know those expectations.

The twelve most common reasons for credit denial based on a credit report are as follows:

1. Delinquent credit obligations.
2. Legal judgments, foreclosures, repossessions..
3. Numerous inquiries.

4. Bankruptcy.

5. Errors in your file.

6. Insufficient credit history.

7. Incomplete application.

8. Length of employment

9. Insufficient income.

10. Excessive obligations.

11. Inadequate collateral.

12. Too short a period of residence.

Delinquent Credit Obligations - This is a leading factor in being turned down for credit. Any late payments in the last 12 months are taken very seriously. If your reasoning is very good, they may extend credit. However, if you run past 30 days late into the 60 or 90 day category, your problems increase. Note: Most creditors want to see 24 months with no late payments.

If you need to miss any payments for income or financial reasons, do so on a priority basis. All major payments—mortgage, rent, MasterCard, Visa, etc.—should be made first. Most people skip the larger payments because it is easier for them, but creditors evaluate you on past history based on larger creditors first.

Legal Judgments, foreclosures, repossessions - a major flaw on your credit. Any outstanding judgment would most likely have to be cleared before any new credit is granted.

Numerous Inquiries - A number of creditors have recently ordered your credit report. This notifies a creditor you are searching for credit and most likely have been turned down by others. Let's say you are a mortgage company and you pull the credit report on a couple and find within the last 30 days two other mortgage companies have inquired about them, but no loan was granted. Were they shopping for the best rate or rejected by the lender? The couple must address each inquiry as to who and what became of the situation. If turned down by other lenders, it will be difficult for them to obtain a loan.

Bankruptcy - While thought by many to be the cure to credit problems, bankruptcy can also be the death to new credit. Twenty-four months after bankruptcy and no late payments, you can apply and obtain a mortgage.

Errors in the File - Errors do happen, and you would know nothing about them until you applied for credit. Review your credit report to find any errors and have them corrected immediately.

Insufficient Credit History - This indicates there is not enough credit information to make a determination. Supplemental credit information needs to be added, such as information from the landlord.

Incomplete Application - The applicant failed to provide information requested. This is easy to appeal, simply reapply to the lender with all requested information.

Length of Employment - Lenders want to see employment stability. Anything less than one year on the job and two years in the same line of work would be inadequate.

Insufficient Income - Lenders use debt ratio to determine if you have sufficient income to cover your debt load.

Excessive Obligations - This is the flip side to lack of income. Your debt to income ratio is out of line. You need to reduce your current monthly obligations before you can obtain more credit.

Inadequate Collateral - The lender is looking for security on the loan and the collateral or asset is less than asked for credit. Auto loans are based on a published book value and real estate loans are based on the appraisal value. The lenders will not grant credit above valuation.

Too Short a Period of Residence - The word again is stability. Lenders view the last 24-36 months. Several moves in this time period are a negative. However, if you are not a home owner and before you were a renter, this would be a positive.

Always examine your credit record before applying for credit. Periodic checking is important because credit bureaus can and do make mistakes in their credit information. They may confuse you with another individual, carry erroneous information in your file, or perhaps include false, incomplete or one-sided information provided by a creditor. Most of these problems can be resolved once you fully understand the procedures.

The Dispute Process

If you find any derogatory item on your credit report that you disagree with such as:

- Unauthorized inquiries
- Collection accounts
- Charge-offs
- Repossessions
- Judgments of liens
- Any negative item you feel is inaccurate

YOU MUST DISPUTE IN WRITING!

To take you through this process, we have created an organized letter campaign to assist you in your dispute action.

NOTE: You must contact all three major credit bureaus for a copy of your report and respond to all three as to the items you wish to dispute. They are all separate and independent reporting agencies, and often, report items differently. One may show a negative item while the other two do not. Since you do not know which report a creditor may be using to check your credit history, you must clear all three.

Most major credit transactions use a three file merged report. This provides information from all three reporting agencies into one comprehensive report. Also, you can go to our website at http//www.pathstoprosperity.info for more free downloadable letters and forms.

Complaint Letter to Delete Inquiries

DATE: (Today's Date)
FROM: (Your Name)
(Your Address)
TO: (Name of Credit Bureau)
(Address of Credit Bureau)

RE: Complaint Letter to Delete Inquiries
Attention: Consumer Relations

I have received a copy of my credit report and find the following items to be inaccurate:

Creditor's Name Account Number Subscriber's I.D. Number ______________ ______________

____

I demand that these inquiries be reinvestigated and deleted from my record. Please send me names and addresses of individuals you contacted so I may follow up.

I shall assume that 30 days constitutes "reasonable time" for verification of these entries unless you immediately notify me otherwise. It should be understood that failure to re-verify these items within 30 days constitutes reason to promptly drop the information from my file according to The Fair Credit Reporting Act of 1970.

Also, please notify me when the items have been deleted. You may send an updated copy of my credit report to the above address. There should be no charge for this information.

Sincerely,

____

Dispute Letter

DATE: (Today's Date)
FROM: (Your Name)
(Your Address)
TO: (Name of Credit Bureau)
(Address of Credit Bureau)

RE: Dispute Letter

Attention: Consumer Relations

I have received a copy of my credit report and find it is inaccurate. A copy of the credit report is attached, where I find inquiries that I did not authorize. The following is a list of those inquiries:

DATE OF INQUIRY	INQUIRER	SUBSCRIBER'S ID #
____________	____________	____________
____________	____________	____________
____________	____________	____________

Please remove these disputed inquiries and send me names and addresses of persons contacted. I shall assume that 30 days constitutes "reasonable time" for verification of these entries unless you immediately notify me otherwise. It should be understood that failure to re-verify within this time constitutes non-verification and these items must be promptly deleted.

Also, please send me notification that the items have been deleted, along with an updated copy of my credit report to the above address. I understand there should be no charge for notification of changes on my credit report.

Sincerely,

____

Second Notice of Dispute

DATE: (Today's Date)
FROM: (Your Name)
(Your Address)
TO: (Name of Credit Bureau)
(Address of Credit Bureau)

RE: Second Notice of Dispute

Attention: Consumer Relations

I have received your notice that you have investigated my dispute and verified that the report will remain unchanged. You have ignored my complaint of reported inaccuracies and these errors have harmed me financially and are continuing to do so. (Describe how you have been financially penalized for this mistake. State what you stand to lose.)

Please correct the problem and send me the names and addresses of all persons contacted.

Again, the inaccurate information is as follows:

____
____
____
____
____
____

If you do not correct these inaccuracies immediately, I will take stronger action. This may include holding you responsible for my financial losses.

Sincerely,

____

Notice of Remaining Errors

DATE: (Today's Date)
FROM: (Your Name)
(Your Address)
TO: (Name of Credit Bureau)
(Address of Credit Bureau)

RE: Notice of Remaining Errors

Attention: Consumer Relations

I have recently received a copy of my updated credit report. I noticed some of the errors have been corrected and others have not. These are still errors: (list unchanged items)

____
____
____
____
____
____

Please re-verify this information and provide me with the names and addresses of those contacted who supplied you this inaccurate information.

Correct this mistake immediately.

Sincerely,

____

Final Letter on Failure to Respond

DATE: (Today's Date)
FROM: (Your Name)
(Your Address)
(Address of Credit Bureau)

RE: Final Letter on Failure to Respond

Attention: Consumer Relations

It has been over 30 days since I sent you a follow-up letter pointing out your failure to respond to my disputes. A photocopy of the letter is attached.

By law, you must respond within a reasonable period of time, and you will also insure the information is fair and equitable to the consumer. Time has come and gone.

You have not provided me with evidence you have acted in a fair and equitable manner, nor have you acted in a reasonable amount of time.

Once again, I am still disputing the information given on my attached letter. I expect a response on or before (Date), otherwise, I will have to contact The Federal Trade Commission.

Please provide me with the names and addresses of all persons you contacted to verify the information.

Sincerely,

____

Demand for Corrected Credit Report

DATE: (Today's Date)
FROM: (Your Name)
(Your Address)
TO: (Name of Credit Bureau)
(Address of Credit Bureau)

RE: Demand for Corrected Credit Report

Attention: Consumer Relations

On (date), I sent a letter stating you have not responded to my request to re-verify the items I had identified as inaccurate or incomplete in my credit report. Photocopies of my letters are attached.

Since you have not provided me with the names of persons you contacted for re-verification of the information, nor have you complied within a "reasonable time" to my request, I assume you have not been able to re-verify the information I have disputed.

I demand you send me a copy of my updated credit report showing the deletion of the items which I disputed on the attached letters. This copy will be at no cost to me. If I do not receive an updated copy of my credit report, with the disputed items deleted, my attorney will pursue my legal rights as to your willful noncompliance.

I have forwarded a copy of this letter to The Federal Trade Commission.

Sincerely,

____

Social Security Number: ______________________________

Request for Release of Credit History

DATE: (Today's Date)
FROM: (Your Name)
(Your Address)
TO: (Name of Creditor)
(Address of Creditor)

RE: Request for Release of Credit History

This letter serves as an authorization and a request to report my good credit history to:

(Name of Credit Bureau)
(Address of Credit Bureau)

I am providing you with information to assist you in locating my account:

My Account Number:

____

My Account Is Under the Name:

____

Thank You,

____

Explanation for Late Payment

DATE: (Today's Date)
FROM: (Your Name)
(Your Address)
TO: (Name of Creditor)
(Address of Creditor)

Dear (Name of Credit Manager),

In reviewing my current credit report, I noticed you have reported my account late on the following dates:

____
____
____

Give detailed reason for late payment.

For the above excusable reason, please correct my payment history of my account at the following credit bureau(s).

(Name & Address of Credit Bureaus)

It is very important to me that my credit report reflects the good relations I have had with your company. Corrections to the report will provide a more representative view of my financial profile.

Thank you for your cooperation.

Sincerely,

____

ACCOUNT NUMBER

____

SOCIAL SECURITY NUMBER

____

Where can you report a debt collector for an alleged violation of the law?

Report any problems you have with a debt collector to your state Attorney General's office and the Federal Trade Commission. Many states also have their own debt collection laws and your Attorney General's office can help you determine your rights.

If you have questions about the Fair Debt Collection Practices Act, or your rights under the Act, write:

Correspondence Branch
Federal Trade Commission
Washington, DC 20580

Although the FTC generally cannot intervene in individual disputes, the information you provide may indicate a pattern of possible law violations.

BEWARE OF CREDIT REPAIR SCAMS

There comes a time in the affairs of men when you must take the bull by the tail and face the situation.
—W.C. Fields

Avoid Credit Repair Clinics

These companies that promise to "fix" your bad credit rating or to erase your bad credit usually are nothing more than ways to take your money. Business is booming among these so-called "credit-repair" companies that charge $100 to more than $1,000 to fix your credit report. In many cases, these outfits take your money and do little or nothing to improve your credit report.

Your credit history is maintained by private reporting companies called credit bureaus that collect information reported to them by banks, mortgage companies, department stores and other creditors. Credit reporting agencies are permitted by law to report bankruptcies for 10 years and other negative information for seven years.

If there are genuine mistakes or outdated items in your report, you can fix them yourself—for free or for only a small amount of money—with little training.

DO NOT FALL FOR ADS LIKE THIS:

Erase Bad Credit	Credit Problems? No problem! 100% guaranteed

Remove bankruptcy and liens from your credit file! A New Credit Identity!

Correcting Errors

You have the right under the Fair Credit Reporting Act, to dispute the completeness and accuracy of information in your credit file. When a credit-reporting agency receives a dispute, it must reinvestigate and record the current status of the disputed items within a reasonable period of time, unless it believes the dispute is "frivolous or irrelevant."

If the agency cannot verify a disputed item, it must delete the item. If your credit report contains erroneous information, the agency must correct the information. If an item is incomplete, the agency must complete it. For example, if your file showed late payments, but failed to show you are no longer delinquent, the agency must show your payments are now current. Or if your file has listed an account that is not yours, the agency would have to delete the account.

Also, at your request, the credit-reporting agency must send a notice of correction to anyone who has checked your file in the past six months.

If a reinvestigation does not resolve your dispute, the Fair Credit Reporting Act permits you to file a statement of up to 100 words to explain your side of the story. That explanation must be included in every report the agency sends.

Registering A Dispute

To dispute information in your credit report, directly notify the credit-reporting agency. Submit your dispute in writing, along with copies (not original) of documents supporting your position. Besides providing your complete name and address, your letter should clearly identify each disputed item. Explain why you dispute the item, and request deletion or correction. You may want to enclose a copy of your report with the questionable items circled.

Send your dispute by certified mail–return receipt requested. Keep copies of your dispute letter and enclosures to document what the agency received.

Adding Accounts to Your File

While most national department store and all-purpose bank credit card accounts will be included in your file, not all creditors supply information to agencies. These may include travel, entertainment, gasoline card companies, local retailers, credit unions, and landlords.

If you were denied credit because of an "insufficient credit file" or "no credit file," and you have accounts not listed in your file, you can ask the credit-reporting agency to add this information to future reports.

Avoid New Credit Identities

If you have filed for bankruptcy, you may be the target of a new credit-repair scheme, often called "file segregation." Here, you are promised a chance to hide unfavorable credit information by establishing a new credit identity. However, there is a problem: File segregation is illegal. If you use it, you could face fines or imprisonment.

You can not avoid your true financial past. Positive new credit and time will repair your situation. If you were able to somehow create a new file that removed the reporting of a bankruptcy and applied for a loan, you may still run into a problem. All loan applications ask the question if you have ever filed for bankruptcy or been foreclosed on. What would happen then? The concept of a new credit file will not help you or work.

Identity Theft Can Destroy You Financially

Identity theft is the act of stealing ones credit information to commit fraud. At the Federal Trade Commission, identity theft is now the Number 1 consumer complaint. It is a crime where only a small percentage of the perpetrators are prosecuted. The problem is there are no witnesses to the crime. No one can testify they actually saw the suspect fill out a credit application.

Anatomy of an ID Theft: How it Begins

You are left with a falling FICO and may face financial ruin. Identity thieves are aggressively seeking your financial information. They are searching the internet to find your information. Another place to capture financial information is in your trash. Yes, your trash holds value to the identity thief. It is filled with your personal account information.

Here is how to protect yourself:

- Stop giving your Social Security number out. Use other types of identifiers first. Social security numbers should be used last and only given to financial institutions you are familiar with or you have contacted.

- Before providing personal identifying information, ask how it will be used and if it will be shared with others. Ask if you can you choose to have it kept confidential.

- Minimize the identification information and the number of cards you carry to what you actually need. If your I.D. or credit cards are lost or stolen, notify the creditors by phone immediately, and place a "lost card alert" on your file.

- Order a copy of your credit report from the three credit reporting agencies every six months. Make sure it is accurate and include only those activities you have authorized.

- Keep items with personal information in a safe place; tear them up when you do not need them anymore. Make sure charge receipts, copies of credit applications, insurance forms, bank checks and statements, expired charge cards, and credit offers you get in the mail are disposed of appropriately.

Your Rights Under The Fair Credit Reporting Act

The Fair Credit Reporting Act (FCRA) protects you against credit abuse that might result in an unfair description of creditworthiness.

1. You have the right to be given the name and address of the consumer reporting agency responsible for preparing a credit report used to deny you credit or employment.

2. You are entitled to a free copy of your credit report within 30 days after notice of credit denial.

3. You are allowed to question the accuracy of your credit report at any time.

4. You have the right to have the reporting agency reinvestigate anything you believe to be incom plete or incorrect information.

5. The credit reporting agency must reinvestigate within a reasonable period of time. The Federal Trade Commission defines *reasonable as immediately unless there is some good reason for the delay.*

6. You are entitled to be given the names and addresses of those who have received a credit report on you within the preceding six months or within the preceding two years if the report was furnished for employment.

7. If the credit bureau cannot confirm the adverse

information or finds any error, it must promptly delete that erroneous information from its files.

8. If the bureau cannot or does not confirm the information you have challenged within a reasonable time period, it also must delete that information from your files.

9. You have the right to have the credit reporting agency notify those you name who have previously received the incorrect or incomplete information that such information has been deleted from your file.

10. If a dispute between you and the reporting agency about information in your credit file cannot be resolved, you have the right to submit a Consumer Statement of your version of the dispute. In other words, if you, as a credit consumer, dispute the accuracy of certain information in your report and receive no satisfaction from the bureau or the creditor, then the credit bureau is required by law to attach your explanation (not to exceed 100 words) to every copy of the report it sends out.

11. You are entitled to have a credit report withheld from anyone who, under the law, does not have a legitimate financial need for the information

12. You have the right not to have adverse information reported after seven years. However, bankruptcy may be reported for ten years.

13. You have the right to sue a credit reporting agency for damages if the agency willfully or negligently violates the law.

GOOD DEBT vs. BAD DEBT

If you want to know your past, look into your present condition. If you want to know your future, look into your present actions.

—Chinese Proverb

It is almost impossible to live debt-free; most of us would never be able to pay cash for our homes. But too many of us let debt get out of hand. Ideally, experts say, your total monthly long-term debt payments, including your mortgage and credit cards, should not exceed 39 percent of your gross monthly income. That's one factor mortgage bankers consider when assessing the creditworthiness of a potential borrower.

It's far too easy to spend more than you can afford, especially when you pay by credit card. The average U.S. household with at least one credit card carries nearly a $9,200 balance, according to CardWeb.com. Personal bankruptcies have hit record highs in recent years.

Of course, avoiding debt at any cost is not smart, either, if it means depleting your cash reserves for emergencies. The challenge is learning how to judge which debt makes sense and which does not, and then wisely managing the money you do borrow.

Good Debt: Three potential areas can be classified as good debt; house, investments, and education. The house is a good debt that offers a positive statement on your credit and your balance sheet. The same should be for investments. Education is considered a good debt, but offers no asset on your balance sheet. In cases where debt makes sense, only take out loans for which you can afford the monthly payments.

Debt is not always a bad thing. In fact, there are instances where the leveraging power of a loan actually helps put you in a better overall financial position.

Buying a home: The chance you can pay for a new home in cash is very small. Carefully consider how much you can afford to put down and how much loan you can carry. The more you put down, the less you will owe and the less you will pay in interest over time. Although it may seem logical to put down every available dime to cut your interest payments, it is not always the best move. You need to consider other issues, such as your need for cash reserves and what your investments are earning.

Also, do not pour all your cash into a home if you have other debt. Mortgages tend to have lower interest rates than other debt, and you may deduct the interest you pay on the first $1 million of a mortgage loan.

Bad Debt: Includes debt you've taken on for primarily consumable items (clothing, food, vacations, entertainment, etc.). The worst form of debt is credit card debt, since it most likely carries the highest interest rates.

6 Points to Remember About Debt

1. Some debt is good. Borrowing for a home or investment property makes good sense. Just make sure you don't borrow more than you can afford to pay back, and shop around for the best terms.

2. Some debt is bad. Do not use a credit card to pay for things you consume quickly, such as entertainment and vacations, if you can't afford to pay off your monthly bill in full. There's no faster way to fall into debt. Instead, put aside some cash each month for these items so you can pay the bill in full.

3. Pay off your highest-rate debts first. The key to getting out of debt efficiently is to first pay down the balances of loans or credit cards that charge the most interest, while paying at least the minimum due on all your other debt. Once the high-interest debt is paid down, tackle the next highest, and so forth.

4. Do not fall into the minimum trap. If you just pay the minimum due on credit-card bills, you

will barely cover the interest you owe, to say nothing of the principal. It will take you years to pay off your balance and potentially you'll end up spending thousands of dollars more than the original amount you charged.

5. Watch where you borrow. It may be convenient to borrow against your home or your retirement account to pay off debt, but it can be hazardous to your financial health. This would put you short of your investing goals in other areas.

6. Do not be so quick to pay down your mortgage. Do not pour all your cash into paying off a mortgage if you have other debt. Mortgages tend to have lower interest rates than other debt, and you may deduct the interest you pay on the first $1 million of a mortgage loan

The Positive Side of Debt

Debt allows you the opportunity to acquire additional assets that can create wealth. Not all debt should be considered negative. In fact, any borrowing for investment purposes is considered positive, for it carries a potential long-term gain. Money borrowed to acquire real estate or purchase a business is a potentially good debt. Any liability that offers a corresponding increase in asset or income generation is a good financial strategy.

Debts fall into two classifications:

1. Secured Debts – Loans that are secured by property of collateral. This collateral guarantees

the creditor the right to take back the property in the case of default of the borrower. Consumer secured loans would be mortgages, auto loans, and equipment loans.

2. Unsecured Debts - No collateral or security. Most debts consumers incur are unsecured. This includes credit cards, department store charges, etc.

Are You Carrying too Much Debt?

Not everything that is faced can be changed, but nothing can be changed until it is faced.

—James Baldwin

The first step is to see if you are trying to maintain debt in excess of your ability to pay. You need to see where you are financially as compared to other consumers.

What is your debt ratio? Are you within a safe debt comfort ratio?

Complete the debt comparison worksheet to see if any area is out of proportion. The major concern is with credit card and installment debts. They are lumped together on this worksheet as one total. Note that housing can be above the averages, because it is counted as positive debt. Any increase in housing expense must come from another area (taxes, installment debt, and living expense).

The two areas taking the first cut back is usually personal savings and gifting. It is unfortunate credit card debt gets priority over savings and gifting. This is an area in need of work. That is why a chapter on wealth accumulation will help. It is hard to complete all the places you want your money to go to when you are simply short of funds. The financial management section will take a deeper look into your cash management.

> *Do what you can, with what you have, where you are.*
>
> —Theodore Roosevelt

Determining Your Debt Comfort Ratio

The most useful way to determine your debt load is to calculate the amount of debt you have in relation to your gross income, commonly referred to as "debt to income ratios."

Debt = Debt Comfort Ratio
Gross Annual Income

This ratio can be figured on a monthly or annual basis. Lenders use the annual method.

Example:

Annual Income

Gross Income	$39,000
Interest/Investment Income	1,000
Other Income	
Total Annual Gross Income	$40,000

Annual Debt Payments

	(Monthly)
Home	$750
Auto	$305
All Credit Cards Minimum Payment	$115
Personal Loan	
All Other Loans	
Total	$1,170

$1,170 x 12 months = $14,040 Annual amount

$$\frac{\$14{,}040}{40{,}000} = 35\%$$

If the ratio is:

25% or less — You are in excellent financial position.

25-33% — A score under 33% is considered, by most financial consultants, to be within the safe financial "comfort ratio."

34-39% — You are considered to be in the median range of the comfort ratio and should be aware any expenditure of increased debt would push you over the ratio.

40-49% — You are now at the high end of the comfort ratio and beginning to become maxed out. You have too

	much debt and must take control of your finances.
50% and over	You are now entering the danger ratio and need to take immediate action to obtain finances within proper ratio. Stop all borrowing or increasing present debt. You need to establish a debt control system and begin reducing debt.

Debt Comparison Worksheet

Another way to evaluate your current debt position is using the debt worksheet on the following page. It helps you compare your situation with a recommended average expense by taking a view of gross income and breaking down what the averages should look like. For example, the largest expense item is housing. The recommended average is 33% of gross income. If your gross income is $4,000 a month, housing should be about $1,330 a month. Remember these are averages and are to be used for comparison points. The range on housing is actually 32% - 41%. This is not a real concern until you exceed the 41% range.

You see I have placed gifting above living expense and savings. Actually it should go right after gross income and ahead of taxes. That is where it should be considered. But for this worksheet, it has to be where it is because unfortunately it is one of the first steps that are reduced to meet other obligations.

The remaining 17% of gross income is allocated

for food, fun, and funding (savings and retirement). So now you can see why Americans save only 1 - 2% of their gross income. This will give you a good idea where you need to make improvements. One of my favorites is reducing the tax category by converting money paid to income taxes into tax friendly retirement plans. This is covered in a later section.

DEBT WORKSHEET
Percentages

Gross Income	100
Estimated Taxes	-20 80% of your income remains
Housing	-33 47% of your income remains
Installment payments	-20 27% of your income remains
Gifting	-10 17% of your income remains
Remaining income for living and savings	

YOUR ACTUAL
Percentages

Gross Income	______________
Estimated Taxes	______________
Housing	______________
Installment Payments	______________
Gifting	______________
Remaining Income	______________

DEBTOR SURVIVAL STRATEGIES

Thou whom avenging powers obey, Cancel my debt (too great to pay), Before the sad accounting day.
—Wentworth Dillon

Your past due notices are piling up and creditors are threatening to turn your account over to a collection agency or even the possibility of a lawsuit. Or worse yet, your creditors may be threatening with:

1. Garnishment of wages
2. Repossession of property
3. Foreclosure of real property
4. Involuntary bankruptcy (where creditors are pushing you in to bankruptcy)

Do not panic! There are several ways to pull yourself out of credit chaos without bankruptcy.

Debt-Solving Remedies without Bankruptcy

Bankruptcy should be a last resort, used only after applying other debt resolution strategies. However, the potential of bankruptcy can be used as a tool to get your creditors to discuss alternative actions.

Four debt-solving strategies:

1. Debt consolidation loans
2. Liquidating assets
3. Negotiate an extended payment plan
4. Compromise the claim

Debt Consolidating Loans

This is a process of having a single larger loan to stretch the debt over a longer pay-back period. The major benefit is the consolidated loan would carry a lower interest rate than the various charge cards and consumer loans you presently have. The second benefit is the payment would be lower because the loan would carry a longer term. If the loan does not meet both of these benefits - don't do it.

The first place to shop for this type of loan would be family and friends. They would be the most likely to know your situation as temporary. The second place to go is finance companies, banks, credit unions, and similar large lenders. You must realize that consolidating all of your loans does not eliminate them. However, it could get you through a period of financial setback and help you get back on course.

Warning: Many unscrupulous lenders make a

business out of exploiting consumers in financial problems. Check on your lender before entering into anything. Do not pay any up-front fees - this is a sure sign of a scam.

Before you proceed with a consolidation loan, review the numbers. Can you reasonably meet the monthly obligation, or are you simply postponing the inevitable? The trade off with the consolidation loan is that your payment term is extended to lower your payment, but since the loan runs for a longer term, your interest expense is greater.

Liquidate Assets

Borrowing is one way to raise funds to pay creditors; another would be to liquidate assets to avoid borrowing. It would be better to sell an asset than to lose it in repossession or ultimately in bankruptcy. With the funds from the sale, you can pay off your creditor.

Methods for raising cash:

- Sell a major asset such as a house or auto. Even if after paying the creditor you have nothing left, you rid yourself of a large monthly obligation.

- Cash in life insurance or tax-deferred account. Life insurance, IRA, or other tax-deferred account may be available. The latter carries a 10% penalty if withdrawn before age 59.

Let us never negotiate out of fear, but let us never fear to negotiate. —John F. Kennedy

Negotiate An Extended Payment Plan

You have now looked at selling property or consolidation borrowing, and still you're trying to find other ways to get out from under your debts. Bankruptcy is still a last resort, but the threat of it can be used to negotiate with your creditors. Once the creditors fear you may file for bankruptcy, you are in a position to negotiate for an extended payment or installment plan.

There are two primary forms of extended or installment plans:

1. Self-administered program
2. Credit counseling plan

With the self-administered program, you contact your creditors with your plan and the threat of bankruptcy as your next step if an extended or installment plan can not be worked out. Most creditors will back down when faced with this option.

Note: This technique applies to unsecured debts only! Real estate mortgages, auto loans, alimony, child support payments, and taxes must be paid and are separate from this plan.

First, make out a realistic budget illustrating your current situation. Use the Debt Liquidation Analysis Form showing your bare needs and what you have left over to work with.

Assume your take-home income is $2,200 per

month and your living expenses are $1,600 per month. You have $600 to pay towards monthly loans which currently are at $850 a month.

The second step is to complete the Debt Consolidation Budget which lists your creditors, what you owe, and how much your monthly payment is.

The third step is to make out the Proposed Debt Payment Plan using the form provided. Using our example of $600 to work with and monthly loan payments of $850, $600 divided by $850 equals .7058. You have coverage of 70% of your current debts. Your proposed payment should be 70% of what they were. With this information, draft a letter to each of your creditor illustrating your current financial situation. Request a temporary reduction of payments. (See sample letter provided.) Make sure your creditors know you plan to pay your account in full. You are asking for their willingness to take a reduced payment over a longer time period.

1. Do not favor one creditor over another. Treat each one equally by paying at set percentage to all creditors.

2. Part of your negotiations is to improve your credit status. Since you are agreeing to pay 100%, request the creditor agree to recognize your plan with an improved credit rating. For example, after three months of punctual payments, a negative rating could be raised to a non-rating status, or after twelve months of punctual payments, the rating is positive.

3. Make sure it is in writing. Once the creditor signs the agreement, if can become part of your credit record.

4. Make the plan conditional upon acceptance by the majority of your creditors. Require at least 85% participation in your plan.

5. Withhold any payments until you receive agreements from your creditors. Why pay before you have an agreement?

6. Do not sign away any of your legal rights. A creditor may request you to sign a confession of judgment as part of the agreement. This way the creditor can get a judgment against you by simply filing the confession with the court and you are precluded from defending the claim. Tell them you will not surrender your constitutional right to trial in the event of a legal suit.

7. Most importantly, honor the agreement once you have a written agreement. You need only to honor it and your credit rating will be restored.

Credit counseling is the second non-bankruptcy strategy for credit work-out. This is a more formalized plan than the self-administered program and creditors might favor this approach. The reason creditors are more inclined to accept a plan sponsored by a Consumer Credit Counseling service is that you are working with a professional they trust to be fair and honest.

Consumer Credit Counseling is a non-profit service. Once they get the plan approved by your creditors, they ask for a donation to support their services. Most creditors support the service.

Note: Do not attempt to get additional credit until you have been in the program for at least 18-24 months and have been current the entire time.

To find the nearest counseling service in your area, look in the Yellow Pages under Credit Counselors. It will be listed as Consumer Credit Counselors of (Name of City). Or write to:

National Foundation for Consumer Credit
1819 H Street
Washington, DC 20006

Compromise Settlements

This is the last alternative before bankruptcy. In fact, this is an out of court settlement based on a pre-bankruptcy result. You must educate your creditors to the fact that you have negligible assets or at least very little, if any, equity. Show your creditor that if you filed for bankruptcy they would get very little, if anything. With your creditors having these facts, you are now ready to negotiate compromise settlement.

A compromise agreement is an actual contract that binds you and your creditors. You must negotiate in good faith. Put yourself in their position. Is your offer fair? Negotiate with your largest creditor first. Without a compromise here, you would have little hope of having success. You need to reach an agreement with the majority of your creditors. Your strategy here is to convince your creditors the agreement is in their best interest.

Present the following benefits:

1. Regular payments, even at a lower amount, are better than irregular, or no payments.

2. Your agreement eliminates collection agency costs or attorney fees that can add up to 50% of the amount they collect.

3. You are making a sincere and fair offer and are not trying to take advantage of the situation.

4. You are taking every step to avoid bankruptcy. If the creditor feels they are receiving more than they would in bankruptcy, they will be more than willing to compromise.

For these reasons, creditors will gladly consider an agreement that offers something to help satisfy their claim.

Debt Settlement Checklist

Reaching a compromise settlement requires both you and your creditors to be flexible. Your creditors goal is simple–they want their money, or as much as possible. As you enter your negotiations, use the following checklist:

1. How much should you offer?

   Like any negotiation, start low. Start with just less than what creditors would receive if you filed bankruptcy. Increase your offer in modest amounts of 5-10%. Do not let your creditor try to strong arm or push you. The key to good negotiating is the attitude of control–knowing the worst case scenario is that you can claim bankruptcy.

2. When should you pay?

   Offer only what you can afford as immediate up-front payment. Future payments should be based on current income with no consideration of greater income in the future.

3. How long should the compromise agreement last?

   Your creditors will want you to make payments until they have recovered their entire claim. Never agree to go over three years. Bankruptcy settlements are only over a three year term. Convince creditors you are unwilling to go past this period and if they insist, let them settle in bankruptcy court.

4. What about returning property?

   Any property that you can return for credit is the same as cash. However, with the return of property, try to get a release for any deficiency balance.

5. What about the rate of interest on the balance?

   Creditors do not receive interest in bankruptcy; however, you are willing to pay a fair rate—prime rate would be reasonable.

6. Can you protect your credit rating?

   This is something you will have to negotiate hard for. You need to fight for the opportunity to preserve or repair your credit rating. Once you have proven you are conforming to the agreement and have a history of timely payments, you can request for improvement of your credit status.

In the following pages you will find sample letters and agreements to assist you in your negotiations with your creditors.

Negotiate, Negotiate, Negotiate - Rather than pay high credit card interest rates call your credit card company and tell them you're planning to move your balance to another company with a lower rate, and then see if they offer you a lower rate to keep you.

Consolidate, Consolidate, Consolidate - Nonprofit services like National Foundation of Consumer Credit or Consumer Credit Counseling Services are available to help consumers consolidate payments and give credit help. Making one payment a month that is less than your total of all separate payments can help consumers work out of their debt.

Sample Letter Proposal to Creditors Seeking Extended Repayment Program

(Date)

Account Number:
Re: Request extended repayment plan

Dear Creditor:

Due to (reason for lack of payments), I have found it impossible to pay my debts as they currently fall due. My current earnings will enable me to meet my obligations, but only if my various creditors are willing to extend the length of my debt by lowering the amount of my monthly payments.

In order to assist you in evaluating my request, I have included three documents as an attachment to this letter. The first attachment, entitled Debt Liquidation Analysis, sets out both my monthly budget for only bare necessities and the amount I have left over. At the present time, I have only $____________ available each month to be applied to my debts.

The second attachment lists all of my creditors, the amount owed to each, and the current monthly payment I am obligated to make to each creditor. (Proposed Debt Payment Plan)

The third attachment shows the amount I propose to make to each creditor. This schedule makes clear that I do not propose to favor any one creditor. Each would receive the same percentage of the $____________ I have available to apply to my total debt. Under my proposal, I would make monthly payments of $____________ to the (name of creditor).

As you review the three attachments to this letter, I am certain you will find my proposal is being made in the utmost of good faith. I am sincerely committed to paying my debts in full, and I know that if you will work with me, your company will be paid in full. I am confident you share my view that your patience in receiving payment is far preferable to a force bankruptcy that would yield little or nothing.

If the plan I have proposed is satisfactory to (creditor), please sign and return the original copy of this letter for my records. I will start making payments under this proposal on the first day of the month following the date you indicate your acceptance of my proposal.

I appreciate your cooperation.

Sincerely,
(Your signature)

Agreed and Accepted:

____

Date: ____________________

Sample Letter Proposal Seeking to Compromise Debt

(Date)
Credit Manager
(Name of Creditor)
(Address of Creditor)
Account Number:

Dear Creditor:

Due to (reason for lack of payments), I am unable to meet my present obligations.

Attached to this letter you will find three schedules. The first attachment, entitled Debt Liquidation Analysis, sets out both my monthly budget for only bare necessities and, additionally, the amount I have left over. At the present time, I take home $____________ above the amount I need for necessities.

The second attachment lists all of my creditors, the amount owed to each, and the current monthly payment I am obligated to make to each creditor. As the schedule indicated, my monthly obligations to my creditors are $____________ , well above the $____________ I have available. Even if all my creditors were willing to grant me extended payback terms, it is clear I simply do not have enough income to offer a realistic payback program.

The third attachment lists the assets against which I can borrow. Based on that schedule, I believe I can raise enough money to pay each of my creditors ______ percent of the money I owe them, if each creditor is willing to accept such a payment as full satisfaction of the amount owed. This offer is being made on the same terms to every creditor listed on the second attachment (entitled Outstand Debt). If accepted by my creditors, I will begin liquidating my assets and will make payments to all of my creditors no later than (date).

I recognize that I am asking my creditors to suffer a loss of ______ cents on every dollar I owe. Frankly, I have no other option. I believe this proposal is more attractive than a forced bankruptcy which would probably provide little or nothing.

If the plan I have proposed is satisfactory to (name of creditor), please sign below and return the original copy of this letter for my records.

Sincerely,

(Your signature)

Agreed and Accepted:

____________________________ Date: ________________

Agreement to Compromise Debt

Be it known, for good consideration, the undersigned as a creditor of (Debtor: You Name) hereby enters into this agreement to compromise and discharge the indebtedness due from the Debtor to the undersigned on the following terms and conditions:

1. The Debtor and the undersigned acknowledge that the present debt due and owing creditor is in the amount of $ ____________.

2. The parties agree that the undersigned creditor shall accept the sum of $ ____________ as full and total payment on said debt and in complete discharge, release, satisfaction and settlement of all monies presently due, provided the sum herein shall be fully and punctually paid in the manner following:

____

____

3. In the event the Debtor fails to fully and punctually pay the compromised amount, the undersigned creditor shall have full rights to prosecute its claim for the full amount of $ ______________ less credits for payments made.

4. In the event of default in payment, the Debtor agrees to pay all reasonable attorneys' fees and costs of collection.

5. This agreement shall be binding upon and inure to the benefit of the parties, their successors, assigns and personal representatives.

Signed under seal this ________ day of __________, 20____.

Witnessed:

______________________________ ______________________________
Creditor

______________________________ ______________________________
Debtor

Agreement to Extend Debt Payment

For value received, the undersigned

_______________(Creditor) and _______________(Debtor) hereby acknowledge and agree that:

1. The Debtor presently owes the Creditor the sum of $_________________: said sum being presently due and payable, but the Debtor is unable to fully pay same at present.

2. In further consideration of the Creditor's willingness to extend the time and manner in which the debt is to be repaid, the Debtor agrees to pay said debt on extended terms in the manner following:

____

____

3. In the event the Debtor fails to make any of the above extended payments on the dates shown above, he shall forfeit all of his rights under this agreement and the Creditor shall have full rights to proceed for the collection of the entire balance then remaining.

4. In the event of default in payment, the Debtor agrees to pay all costs of collection, including reasonable attorneys' fees.

5. This agreement shall be binding upon and inure to the benefits of the parties, their successors, assigns and personal representatives.

Signed under seal this ________ day of ___________, 20____.

____

Creditor

____

Debtor

General Release

Be it known, for good consideration, the undersigned hereby jointly and severally forever releases, discharges, acquits and forgives ___________________ from any and all claims, actions, suits, demands, agreements, liabilities and proceedings of every nature and description both at law and in equity arising from the beginning of time to the date of these presence and more particularly related to an incident that arose out of:

____

____

____

This release shall be binding upon and inure to the benefit of the parties, their successors, assigns and personal representatives.

Signed under seal this _________ day of ___________, 20____.

Witnessed:

____________________ ___________________________

____________________ ___________________________

Debt Repayment Plans

If your financial difficulties arise from too much debt or an inability to repay your debts, a credit counseling agency may work out a Debt Repayment Plan for you. In these plans, you deposit money each month with the credit counseling agency. Your deposits are used to pay your creditors according to a payment schedule the counselor develops with you.

As part of the repayment plan, you may have to agree not to apply for—or use—any additional credit while you're participating in the program. A successful repayment plan requires you to make regular, timely payments, and could take 48 months or longer to complete. Some credit counseling agencies charge little or nothing for managing the plan; others charge a monthly fee that could add up to a significant charge over time.

A debt repayment plan does not erase your credit history. Under the Fair Credit Reporting Act, accurate information about your accounts can stay on your credit report for up to seven years. A bankruptcy can stay on your report for ten years. In addition, your creditors will continue to report information about accounts that are handled through a debt repayment plan. For example, creditors may report that an account is in financial counseling, that payments have been missed, or that there are write-offs or other concessions. But a demonstrated pattern of timely payments should help you get credit in the future.

Secured and Unsecured Debt

Your debts are either secured or unsecured.

Secured debts usually are tied to an asset, like your car for a car loan or your house for a mortgage. If you stop making payments, the lender can repossess your car or foreclose on your house. Unsecured debts are not tied to any asset. Examples include most credit card debt, bills for medical care, signature loans and debts for other types of services. Debt repayment plans usually cover only your unsecured debt. If your secured debts are not included in the plan, you must continue to make payments to these creditors directly.

When you borrow money to buy a car, the lender generally holds the title to the car until the debt is paid in full. Most automobile financing agreements allow the lender to repossess your car if you stop making payments. No notice is required. If your car is repossessed, you may have to pay the full balance due on the loan, as well as towing and storage costs, to get it back. If not, the lender may sell the car, perhaps for less than what you still owe. You are still responsible for the difference. If you fall behind with your car payments, consider working with the holder of the title of your car to sell it yourself. Pay off the debt to avoid repossession and a negative entry on your credit report.

If you fall behind on your mortgage, contact your lender immediately to avoid foreclosure. Most lenders will work with you if they believe you're acting in good faith and the situation is temporary. Some lenders may reduce or suspend your payments for a short time. When you resume regular payments, you may have to pay extra toward the past due total. Lenders may agree to change the terms of the mortgage by extending the repayment period to reduce the monthly payments. Ask about any fees charged for these changes, and consider how much they add to the total cost of your loan.

If you and your lender cannot work out a plan, contact a housing counseling agency. Some agencies limit their counseling services to homeowners with FHA mortgages, but many offer free help to any homeowner having trouble making mortgage payments. Call the local office of the Department of Housing and Urban Development (HUD) or the housing authority in your state, city, or county for help in finding a housing counseling agency near you.

Choosing an Agency: Questions to Ask

If you want to work with a credit counseling agency, interview several. Here are some questions to ask. Check with your state Attorney General, local consumer protection agency and the Better Business Bureau to find out if consumers have filed complaints about the provider you are considering. Any reputable credit counseling agency should send you free information about itself and the services it provides without requiring you to provide any details about your situation. If not, consider that as a red flag and go elsewhere for help.

Service Fees

- What services do you offer?
- In addition to helping me solve my immediate

problem, will you help me develop a plan for avoiding problems in the future?

- What are your fees? Do I have to pay anything before you can help me? Are there monthly fees? What's the basis for the fees?

- What is the source of your funding?

- Will I have a formal written agreement or contract with you?

- How soon can you take my case?

- Will I work with one counselor or several?

- What are the qualifications of your counselors? Are they accredited or certified? If not, how are they trained?

- What assurance do I have that information about me (including my address and phone number) will be kept confidential?

Repayment Plan

- How much do I have to owe to use your services?

- How do you determine the amount of my payment? What happens if this is more than I can afford?

- How does your debt repayment plan work? How

will I know my creditors have received payments? Is client money put in a separate account from operating funds?

- How often can I get status reports on my accounts? Can I get access to my accounts online or by phone?

- Can you get my creditors to lower or eliminate interest and finance charges or waive late fees?

- Is a debt repayment plan my only option?

- What if I can not maintain the agreed-upon plan?

- What debts will be excluded from the debt repayment plan?

- Will you help me plan for payment of these debts?

10

FORECLOSURE: THE REAL FINANCIAL FEAR FACTOR

Riches do not consist in the possession of treasures, but in the use made of them.

—Napoleon I

By now, you know the seriousness of credit problems facing consumers today. Foreclosure is the top of the credit chaos scale. In the last twenty years the number of foreclosures has increased over 300 percent. In my hometown of Kansas City, we publish the KC Foreclosure Monitor that tracks the number of foreclosures filed. In a typical month for the five counties included in the report, there is an average of 500-600 foreclosures filed. That is over 6,000 a year in one metropolitan area. This is an astonishing number of foreclosures considering in 1980, the total nation wide number was 112,000. The sad thing is I do not see the number of foreclosures reducing in the next few years.

The reasons are many. At the top is the easy access to credit, lax lending policies, and in the case of foreclosures, the cash out loans which are stripping consumers of their equity, as well as the problem of predatory lending. For many, the cause for the foreclosure is loss of job, divorce, health issues, and even the death of a spouse.

The truly sad part is most people in foreclosure feel there is nothing they can do, or there is no way out of this desperate situation. They are being inundated with mailings and calls from the investment vultures wanting to take what equity remains.

The two types of foreclosure actions used to foreclose on deeds of trust loans and mortgages are:

1. Judicial
2. Non-judicial

To find your state's foreclosure statute you can go online and enter your state name followed by Foreclosure Statute or call your local county courthouse.

Judicial Foreclosure

The judicial foreclosure is where the foreclosing lender files a lawsuit. The process by which the property is foreclosed is a six-step procedure.

Step 1. Delinquency

At this point, the borrower has failed to make the payment. The lender sends a delinquent letter and if the delinquency is not paid, it goes into default. If no payments are made, the lender refers it to an attorney to send a default letter. The letter usually demands immediate payment in full of all delinquent amounts and advises the borrower if payment is not received by a set date, a suit will be filed to foreclose on the property.

Step 2. *LIS Penden*

LIS Penden is considered "legal notice" a suit has been filed which affects the title of the property.

Step 3. Complaint

The complaint sets forth the plaintiff and defendant, and goes into detail as when the loan was created and how much money is in default. The borrower has the opportunity to respond to the complaint, and a court date is set.

Step 4. Final judgment

If the default has not been cured, the plaintiff (lender) can file a motion for final judgment. Curing the default means paying all back payments, late fees, and costs. The final judgment documents the inactions of the defendant (borrower), allowing the plaintiff to take action. This sets the stage for the Motion of Sale.

Step 5. Sale

Once the judge signs the Motion for sale, a date is set on which the property will be sold at public auction. The borrower may exercise any statutory redemption rights after sale.

Step 6. Redemption Period

Some states provide a statutory redemption

period that is a time after the auction sale the borrower can redeem the property by paying all due under the defaulted payments and fees. A sheriff's deed or certificate of title is given to the highest bidder after the statutory redemption period expires.

Non-Judicial Foreclosure

States where non-judicial foreclosures occur, the foreclosing lender or deed of trust beneficiary invokes the power of sale covenant. Typically under the power of sale foreclosure the following happens:

1. The trustee sends a letter informing the grantor or property owner they are in default and demands immediate payment.

2. The trustee files a notice of default with the county in which the property is located.

3. The public trustee's sale date is set and the property is advertised it will be sold at public auction.

4. The property is sold to the highest bidder at the trustee's public auction.

5. The borrower may exercise any statutory redemption rights.

6. A trustee's deed is issued to the highest bidder.

After the sale, the highest bidder will usually file

for an eviction to anyone residing in the property. Many times, the resident is an unsuspecting renter, who had no idea of the default and foreclosure.

Know Your Options

Forbearance

Forbearance is an agreement between the lender and the borrower to reinstate the delinquent loan through the payment of a set amount and schedule of payments over a period of time. If a borrower is behind in his or her payment by $4,000, for example, the lender may allow the borrower to pay the money back through installment payments over six months to a year. The lender may decide on the other hand to allow the borrower to pay a reduced monthly payment until the borrower has an opportunity to get back on their feet and pay any remaining arrearages in one lump sum.

The forbearance usually is a written agreement between the lender and the borrower. Generally, these agreements will not exceed more then 18 – 24 months.

Loan Modification

A loan modification is a change in any of the terms of the original note. This includes decreasing the interest rate, extending the term of the loan, or other options at the lender's discretion to assist the borrower through a temporary set back.

Generally a lender will consider a loan modification when foreclosure is eminent. The borrower must be able to demonstrate they have the ability to keep the loan current after the loan modification.

Sale to Preserve Equity

Your home has equity if its value is worth more than you owe on your mortgage. If due to financial adversity (i.e. loss of income, divorce, unemployment, medical bills, etc.) you can no longer make your monthly mortgage payments, your immediate goal is to try to sell your home and find more affordable housing.

However, time may not be on your side. If you default on your mortgage payments, you risk having your lender initiate foreclosure and losing your home and its equity. Under this pressure you may have to settle for selling your home for less than you could if you had more time.

Repayment Plan

A repayment plan is suited to a homeowner who has had a financial hardship but is now getting back on their feet and wants to bring their delinquent mortgage current. Although you are recovering, you are probably several months (and thus several thousand dollars) behind on your mortgage payments and need time to repay what you owe. When you contact your lender, the lender's collections department will probably demand an aggressive repayment schedule to avoid foreclosure. Paying back your delinquent mortgage payments under those terms could jeopardize your chances of recovering financially.

Second Mortgage – or additional financing

A lender may offer a second loan or junior lien to a borrower in order to make up any back payments, late fees and other charges necessary to reinstate the loan. The borrower in return, will be required to make an additional mortgage payment to cover the principal and interest payments on the second loan. Interest rates often rival credit cards and should be looked at with caution.

Mortgage Refinancing

Mortgage refinancing is an option where the lender would allow the borrower to refinance their existing mortgage, adding in the late payments and fees in the loan to allow the borrower to retain the property.

Pre-foreclosure – Short Sale

"Short Sale" is where the lender agrees to settle the loan for less than the outstanding balance owed. To conduct a short sale a third party (company or realtor) negotiates with your lender(s) to allow you to sell your home to pay back your loan(s) at a discounted amount. All costs for the sale are paid for by the sale itself.

With a pre-foreclosure short sale, the homeowner can avoid damaging their credit rating any further and has the peace of mind of getting out of their mortgage debt. Consequently short sales are most appealing to homeowners who have little or no equity in their property. They would be unable to sell their home without coming to the closing with money "out of pocket."

Debt Liquidation Analysis

BARE NECESSITIES ONLY

	PER MONTH:
RENT/MORTGAGE	$_______________
TRANSPORTATION (Gas, Auto Payments, Etc.)	$_______________
FOOD	$_______________
CLOTHING	$_______________
UTILITIES (Gas, Electric, Telephone, Water)	$_______________
INSURANCE (Auto, Life, Health, Medical)	$_______________
CHILD CARD	$_______________
OTHER:	
______________________________	$_______________
______________________________	$_______________
______________________________	$_______________
______________________________	$_______________
TOTAL BARE NECESSITIES	$_______________
MONTHLY INCOME AFTER TAXES	$_______________
AMOUNT LEFT FOR DEBT REDUCTION	$_______________
(AMOUNT SHORT)	$_______________

Debt Consolidation Budget

CREDITOR (who you owe)	BALANCE WHAT YOU OWE	MONTHLY PAYMENT

Net Asset Borrowing Chart			
ASSET:	CURRENT FAIR MARKET VALUE	LOAN AGAINST ASSET	NET EQUITY
REAL ESTATE:			
	$	$	$
	$	$	$
	$	$	$
AUTOMOBILES:			
	$	$	$
	$	$	$
STOCKS, BONDS, MUTUAL FUNDS:			
	$	$	$
	$	$	$
	$	$	$
	$	$	$
BUSINESS INTEREST:			
	$	$	$
	$	$	$
	$	$	$
PERSONAL PRPERTY:			
	$	$	$
	$	$	$
	$	$	$
OTHER ASSETS:			
	$	$	$

Proposed Debt Payment Plan			
CREDITOR	TOTAL AMOUNT OWED	CURRENT MONTHLY PAYMENT	PROPOSED MONTHLY PAYMENT
	$	$	$
	$	$	$
	$	$	$
	$	$	$
	$	$	$
	$	$	$
	$	$	$
	$	$	$
	$	$	$
	$	$	$
	$	$	$
	$	$	$
	$	$	$
	$	$	$
	$	$	$
	$	$	$
	$	$	$
	$	$	$
	$	$	$
	$	$	$
	$	$	$
	$	$	$
	$	$	$
	$	$	$
	$	$	$
	$	$	$
	$	$	$
	$	$	$
	$	$	$
	$	$	$
	$	$	$
	$	$	$
	$	$	$
	$	$	$
	$	$	$
	$	$	$
	$	$	$
	$	$	$
	$	$	$

I was going to buy a copy of 'The Power of Positive Thinking,' and then I thought: What the heck good would that do?

—Ronnie Shakes

Quick Cash Analysis

Analysis as of ____________________

Primary Source of Immediate Cash:

Checking	$ ____________
Savings	$ ____________
Money Market	$ ____________
Credit Card Limits	$ ____________
TOTAL	$ ____________

Secondary Sources of Cash:

Loan on Cash Value of Life Insurance	$ ____________
Loan from Profit-Sharing Plan	$ ____________
Early Withdrawal from Pension or IRA	$ ____________
Sell of Personal Assets	$ ____________
Second Mortgage or Equity Loan	$ ____________
Loan from Bank	$ ____________
Loan from Friends or Family	$ ____________
TOTAL	$ ____________
TOTAL FROM BOTH SOURCES	$ ____________

Review of Chapters on Credit

What is your credit card debt in comparison to the average household?

What is your FICO score (this is for you alone)?

Where does your FICO Score fall?

Are you in the top 50% quatrain or the lower?

Calculate your debt comfort ratio.

Are changes needed?

What are your thoughts on good debt vs. bad debt?

Identity theft is becoming a large financial fear. How can you protect yourself?

What debt-solving strategies can you use to avoid bankruptcy?

Once a foreclosure has been filed, what can be done?

FINANCIAL MANAGEMENT

The way of a fool seem right to him, but a wise man listens to advice (Proverbs 12:15).

This book is based on over 25 years of teaching and consulting on wealth management. When I was a professor of finance, the school added the Certified Financial Planner (CFP) program. I found the program to be a much needed curriculum and was something truly missing in any educational program. This was a great program for those wanting to enter the field of financial management. Accountants, stockbrokers, insurance agents, and mutual fund representatives were enrolling in the Certified Financial Planner program. But I could not help but feel something was missing. It was designed for those who already had money. Still there were two areas not addressed in the program at the time. The area needing greater coverage was credit and secondly how to truly accumulate wealth.

I joined the board of The American Finance Institute to develop a course for credit and financial management. This became a ministry of sort, for me. I found people suffering from the lack of credit and financial education and the course began improving their lives. After a few years, those who took the first course were now asking about going to the next level, the accumulation of wealth phase. A proven program of wealth building was added and has been used since 1979. A system not based on complicated formulas or carrying high risk, but one that has created hundreds of very prosperous people. The wealth skills will give you the opportunity to create your own financial prosperity.

The path to prosperity will require you to apply some effort to your financial growth. The process is not complicated, but will require your time.

This is where you will run into a couple of stumbling blocks:

1. Resistance & Avoidance

2. Fear and Self-Doubt

Most people resist working on their financial situation because they fear that it takes too much time and energy. Fear and self-doubt paralyze action by ones lack of confidence or fear of failure. Many people cling to the belief that someone else will handle it for them.

The choice is yours. The bottom-line question: Do you pursue what could be or do you accept where you are? Again, most choose to do nothing, be it fear, time or lack of training - who knows? This we do know. Fear is interest paid on a debt you may not owe.

The reason many people feel fear is based on their lack of knowledge. They are dependent on having someone else handle their finances, thus giving control to someone else.

If you continue doing what you have always done, you will get what you have always gotten. If you want to be financially successful, you must take control over your financial education and investment management.

> *Wisdom is a shelter as money is a shelter, but the advantage of knowledge is this: that wisdom preserves the life of its possessor* (Ecclesiastes 7:12).

Financial Literacy

> *Two roads, diverged in a wood, and I took the one less traveled by, and it has made all the difference.*
> —Robert Frost

When people leave school, be it high school, college, or graduate school, they are most likely credit and financially illiterate. I can not put enough emphasis on the importance of credit and financial literacy.

The job of learning credit and finance is left to trial and error or learned as you go. Many receive their basic training from their parents or friends. And that is why those who have not been trained in terms of credit and finance fall prey to those who do have knowledge. Millions if not billions of dollars are lost each year due to the lack of credit and financial literacy. According to Robert Kiyosaki in his book, *Rich Dad's Guide to Investing*, "I believe that the lack of financial education is why nine out of ten new businesses fail in the first five years, and why most investors think investing is risky and do not make or keep much money."

Most investors can be divided into three groups:

Quick to Act
Slow to Act
Unable to Act

The "quick to act" persons are able to pull the trigger on a deal very quickly based on two different theories. The first, person is blessed with years of experience. The second person is one who acts based on the following, "sounds good let's do it" philosophy. The first will make money most of the time. The second may get lucky, but in the long run will lose. The latter should stick with buying lottery tickets because that is how they handle their finances.

"Slow to act" describes a person willing to take the time to analyze the numbers, the investment, the people involved, and project, and the expected return. Some of the "slow to act" become so bogged down in the analyzing phase they keep examining the numbers until the investment is no longer available. They are simply getting ready to get ready.

The last group, falling in the category of "unable to act," have no idea what the numbers mean or how to calculate an expected amount of return. They are financially challenged to the point of being frozen and are unable to move ahead.

The process of due diligence or research can be slow at first. Due diligence simply means–discovering what is fact and what is fiction. When it comes to investments most people are searching for ways to shortcut the due diligence process. On the other hand you have those who research and question every minimal issue to the point of reaching "analysis paralysis." Over time the process becomes faster, easier, and more exciting. Again we can define the three investment modes by using an old cliché: "Those who know what's happening, those who would like to know what's happening and those who say, "what happened?"

The quicker you are able to complete your due diligence on an investment, the more likely you will find the investment with the highest expected safety, cash flow and over all return.

FINANCIAL PLANNING BASICS

If you would be wealthy, think of saving rather than getting.

—Benjamin Franklin

Think of a financial plan as a road map. It helps you develop and define your short, intermediate and long-term goals, take stock of where you are today and map a path to get you to your goals.

It is important to remember that financial planning is a process, not a product. Life and circumstance change, so your financial plan will need to be reviewed and revised on a regular basis.

There are a number of steps to the financial planning process including:

1. Evaluate your current situation.

2. Review your insurance coverage.

3. If you have children, develop a *college funding* plan to help cover higher education expenses.

4. Review your current tax situation to identify tax-saving opportunities.

5. Develop a **retirement funding** plan that covers when you plan to retire and how much you will need to support your retirement lifestyle.

6. Review your estate plan to ensure that your will, living will, healthcare power of attorney and other **estate planning** documents (revocable living trusts and durable power of attorney) are up-to-date and valid.

7. Develop an overall **investment or wealth accumulation plan.**

8. Finally, review your plan and progress periodically by giving yourself an annual check up to make sure you are staying on track.

Always bear in mind that your own resolution to success is more important than any other one thing.
—Abraham Lincoln

The Way to Succeed

We face a challenge in developing a new financial mind-set. We know our present course is unacceptable, and we truly want to achieve some form of financial excellence. The following steps will help you to succeed:

1. Current Financial Assessment - A discovery of where you are currently. Your goals and

dreams become the base of the system. The processes and tools are a method of organizing and controlling your resources; they are the tools to attaining wealth.

2. Setting Financial Objectives - Clearly identifying both your short-term and long-term financial aspirations.

3. Implementation of a Proven System - A step-by-step guide can be applied and mastered in developing strategies and results measured.

4. Monitor Your Plan - A periodic review to determine if any changes in your financial strategy are needed.

Actually, I have no regard for money. Aside from its purchasing power, it's completely useless as far as I'm concerned. —Alfred Hitchcock

How to Get Started

Successful financial management involves two critical steps, knowledge of the financial world and the ability to build assets through saving. It is impossible to accumulate wealth and keep it without both of these steps. Smart investors, no matter what assets they have, will invest as much as possible. Regardless of how much you make, if you fail to monitor your finances, you will not become financially secure.

A budget is telling your money where to go instead of wondering where it went.

—John C. Maxwell

No Budget Needed

Most financial books you pick up start with the advice of budgeting. A recent survey found 70% of Americans do not use a budget, and of the 30% who claim to keep a budget, two-thirds of them admit that they do not stay within the parameters. Why do budgets fail, or better yet, why bother?

The number one reason for budget failure is it requires a lot of hard work and discipline over an extended period of time. Budgets are like financial diet plans, most wait until they are heavily burdened with debt before trying to regulate their spending habits. They view their flabby financial figure and decide to snap it into shape with a strict financial diet. Robert Frost knew budgets did not work when he wrote: "Nobody was ever meant to remember or invent what he did with every cent." After years of budgetary neglect, you can not expect to achieve fast financial fitness. There are no overnight miraculous exercises to riches. But by following the advice set forth, you can make substantial progress in a little time.

So if the budget is not the place to start, then where do we begin? Focus on your net worth.

I started out with nothing. I still have most of it.
—Michael Davis

Net Worth

Begin with your net worth. Where are you today financially? Evaluate your net worth using the net worth test to see how you compare to others based on age and income.

Net Worth

ASSETS

ACCOUNTS	VALUE
Checking	$ ________
Savings	$ ________
Money Markets	$ ________
U.S. Savings Bonds	$ ________
INVESTMENT ACCOUNTS	
Stocks	$ ________
Bonds	$ ________
Mutual Funds	$ ________
Certificates of Deposit	$ ________
Real Estate Owned	$ ________
IRA's Vested Pensions and Profit Sharing	$ ________
401K's	$ ________
Annuities	$ ________
Life Insurance (Cash Value)	$ ________
Notes Receivable	$ ________
Business Interest	$ ________
PERSONAL ASSETS	
Auto's	$ ________
Collections	$ ________
Household Goods (Furniture & Accessories)	$ ________
Other	$ ________
TOTAL ASSETS	$ ________

LIABILITIES	AMOUNT OWED
Current Bills Outstanding	$ ________
Credit Card Balances	$ ________
Mortgages	$ ________
Auto Loans	$ ________
Boat Loans	$ ________
Personal Loans	$ ________
Educational Loans	$ ________
Installment Loans	$ ________
Other Debts	$ ________
TOTAL LIABILITIES	$ ________
TOTAL ASSETS	$ ________
MINUS TOTAL LIABILITIES	$ ________
NET WORTH	$ ________

This is the best place to start any financial planning. Where are you? Are you in need of a financial makeover or are you already above average? The net worth test gives us an estimate of how well you are doing financially

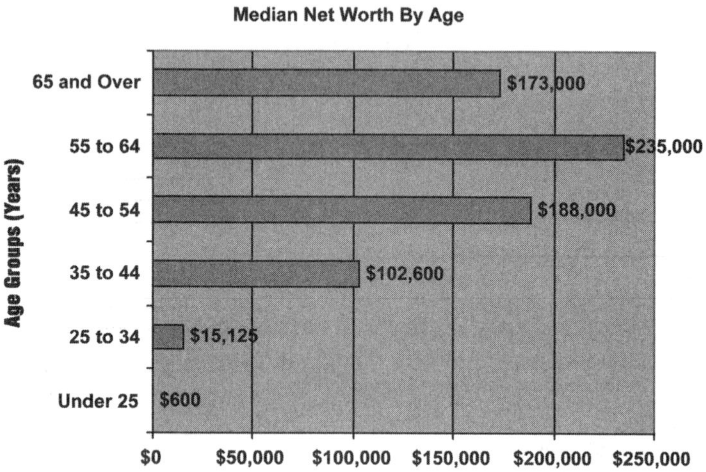

WHO HAS WHAT...Here's the percentage of American households that have achieved various levels of net worth.

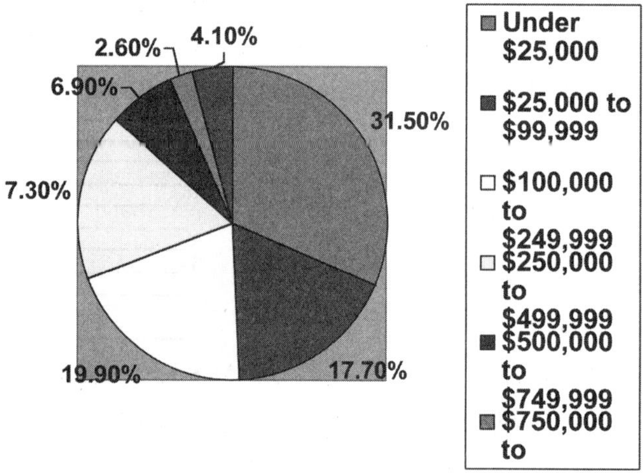

31.5%	Net Worth under $ 25,000
17.7%	Net Worth $25,000 - $99,999
19.9%	Net Worth $100,000 - $249,000
7.30%	Net Worth $250,000 - $499,999
6.9%	Net Worth $500,000 - $749,999
2.6%	Net Worth $750,000 - $999,999
4.1%	New Worth $1,000,000 and up

WHERE ARE YOU, REALLY

Even if you're on the right track, you'll get run over if you just sit there.

—Will Rogers

Take the Net Worth Test

	Your Numbers	Example
1. Your household income		65,000
2. Your age (average husband & wife age)	______	40
3. Multiply your income by your age	______	2,600,000
4. Multiply by the factor of .07	______	182,000
5. Your current net worth	______	200,000
6. Your score: Divide line 5 by line 4	______	1.10
	______	

What the score means for your age:

.50 and below	You are in need for a financial makeover.
.51 - .99	You are below average and need to make improvements.
1.00	You are at the medium for your age.
1.10 – 1.49	You are above average.
1.50 – 2.00	You are in the top 30% of wealth builders.
2.1 and above	You are in the top 15% of wealth builders.

I always wanted to be somebody, but I should have been more specific.

—Lily Tomlin

1. Your net worth is less than your total annual inflow. What do you mean *less*? It may even be negative. Welcome to the majority. This section will show you how to develop a plan to increase your net worth and invest.

2. Your net worth is more than one year's annual inflow but less than four year's. If you are under 40 and own your own home plus other appreciating assets, you're in good shape. If not, you need to accelerate your investment profile.

3. Your net worth is more than four year's inflow, but less than ten year's. If you are under 50, you are probably on course.

4. Your net worth is more than ten times your annual inflow. You are ahead of the game. Enjoy it. You deserve it.

5. Another comparison would be to compute your asset-to-debt ratio. Divide the total assets by the total liabilities.

If, for example, your assets are $120,000 and your liabilities total $40,000, then your asset-to-debt ratio is 3 to 1.

The recommended asset-to-debt ratio is as follows:

Age:	25-34	1.5 to 1
	35-44	2 to 1
	45-54	3.5 to 1
	55-64	5 to 1
	65 & over	7 to 1

You can see that in the later years the asset base is increasing considerable due to two major factors:

1. Growth or appreciation of assets
2. Debt reduction

A classic example would be the purchase of a home at age 25 for $90,000 on a 30 year mortgage with 20% down. This asset carries a ratio of 1.25 to 1.

$72,000 mortgage; $90,000 value

$$\frac{90{,}000}{72{,}000} = 1.25$$

In ten years, the loan balance is at $64,400.

$64,400 mortgage; $90,000 value

$$\frac{90{,}000}{64{,}400} = 1.398$$

Lack of money is the root of all evil.

—George Bernard Shaw

THE FLOW OF FUNDS

Your future is whatever you make it, so make it a good one.

—Doc, *Back to the Future III*

You need a very clear awareness of how money flows into your life. To put it simply, you need to know where it comes from and where it goes. In order to know this, you need to pay attention and keep track of the flow of funds.

To begin with you need to start with and understand the flow of funds. Yes, money has its own path and I know what you are thinking, you are either on the wrong path, a path paved with too many obstructions or the path just seems too long.

The flow of funds outlines how money travels in and out of your life. There are two primary ways funds flow in:

1. Funds you earn from work.

2. Funds you receive from returns on your money like interest or dividends.

As funds flow down the path choices must be made as to its direction. You have three choices with those funds.

1. To gift it
2. To live on it
3. To invest it

To put it another way, you can:

1. Share It
2. Spend It
3. Save It

The first choice is "gift it." Establish a planned giving program. Set aside funds weekly or monthly and stick with your plan.

> *Each man should give what he has decided in his heart to give, not reluctantly or under compulsion, for God loves a cheerful giver* (2 Corinthians 9:7).

The key here is setting a standard of giving, such as tithing, can help us do what we believe in our hearts to be right. It should be a free and joyous decision.

Most people handle their funds a little different. They spend most of it, save some of it, and share little of it—if any. We live in a spending society where the incoming funds are not the end of the spending. Easy credit helps consumers mortgage their financial future.

Our focus must be on converting as many funds as possible to the investment stage. Once we have funds to invest, we must concentrate on their growth. Most people focus their attention on an investment product, not on an investment plan. Investing needs a plan, a plan to go from where you are to where you want to be. In fact investing is not what most people think it is. They think investing requires a special knowledge, a high degree of risk, luck and knowing—what's hot. Investing requires some knowledge, but no special secret training only a few have. This misconception convinces some they must entrust their money and faith to someone they pray knows what they are doing. Investing is a procedure, a plan, a path to prosperity. Becoming prosperous is automatic if you follow the right plan.

One of the best places to expand your investment knowledge is to first look at the most common investment mistakes others make.

15 Leading Investment Mistakes People Make

1. Procrastinating about your personal investment plan.

2. Not investing enough. The average personal savings rate is now less than 2% of income.

3. Not doing your own due diligence: researching and studying before investing.

4. Taking too much (or too little) risk.

5. Being an optimist when the market is high and a pessimist when it is low.

6. Using the "comeback theory," holding investments when they are down in hope they will come back to a profitable position.

7. Acquiring investments based solely on tips. Chasing what's hot.

8. Focusing too much on yield and not knowing what "high" yield means. High yield means increased risk.

9. Having no financial plan or investment strategy, or having a plan and not following it in both good times and in bad.

10. Over concentration. Too much in the company you work for or in the industry you work in.

11. Overtrading and ignoring expenses. But frequent traders yield less than buy and hold investors.

12. Falling in love with an investment. Refusing to recognize when to sell an asset.

13. Attending one too many "no money down" seminars. Not recognizing potential risks. Creating an overly leveraged position.

14. Being too greedy. Always shooting for the moon. Going for the big kill, usually ends up killing your financial position in the long run.

15. Mismanaging retirement accounts–nearly half of all retirement plan participants who change jobs fail to roll over their accounts.

These are fifteen investment mistakes that you should focus on because they are the ones most likely to cost you in the long run. There is nothing particularly esoteric about any of these mistakes. Most of them begin in ordinary understandable human tendencies. That does not make them easy to avoid, but it does mean you do not have to have an MBA in finance to correct them.

If you are guilty of any of these mistakes, start yourself on the road to fixing them. Between your retirement plan at work, your IRAs and other taxable investments, you should be putting aside 10% of your gross income up to age 40, 15% up to age 55, and 20% up to retirement. Anything less than this amount and you are not in the game to succeed. The increase at various ages is vital to your plan. At an 8% return, every dollar saved at age 30 is worth more at retirement than three dollars saved at age 50. If you are not anywhere near these saving targets, you must increase either the amount saved or the amount of return. The real key to managing assets is being disciplined to "a hands off policy." That means not spending assets or using them for anything other than future needs.

CASH FLOW/INCOME WORKSHEET

INCOME	MONTHLY	ANNUAL
Salary	$__________	$__________
Commission	$__________	$__________
Bonuses	$__________	$__________
Alimony & Child Support	$__________	$__________
Interest	$__________	$__________
Dividends	$__________	$__________
Rents & Royalties	$__________	$__________
Partnership Distributions	$__________	$__________
Pensions	$__________	$__________
Other Income	$__________	$__________
TOTAL CASH AVAILABLE	$__________	$__________

CONTINUE ON
NEXT PAGE

CASH FLOW/INCOME WORKSHEET (continued)

OUTGO USES OF INCOME	MONTHLY	ANNUAL
Rent/Mortgage Payment	$________	$________
Total Utilities	$________	$________
Maintenance	$________	$________
Property Taxes	$________	$________
Home or Renter's Insurance	$________	$________
Auto Payments	$________	$________
Gas	$________	$________
Auto Repairs	$________	$________
Auto Insurance	$________	$________
Credit Card Payments	$________	$________
Installment Loans	$________	$________
Insurance Premiums	$________	$________
Life	$________	$________
Health	$________	$________
Disability	$________	$________
Income Taxes	$________	$________
Food	$________	$________
Entertainment	$________	$________
Clothing	$________	$________
Child Care	$________	$________
Education	$________	$________
Vacation	$________	$________
Contributions	$________	$________
Alimony/Child Support	$________	$________
Other Payments	$________	$________
TOTAL EXPENSES	$________	$________

SEE NEXT PAGE
FOR ANALYSIS

CASH FLOW/INCOME COMPARISON

OUTGO USES OF INCOME	PROJECTED	ACTUAL	(+ OR -)
Rent / Mortgage Payment	$	$	$
Total Utilities	$	$	$
Maintenance	$	$	$
Property Taxes	$	$	$
Home/Renter's Insurance	$	$	$
Auto Payments	$	$	$
Gasoline	$	$	$
Auto Repairs	$	$	$
Auto Insurance	$	$	$
Credit Card Payments	$	$	$
Installment Loans	$	$	$
Insurance Premiums			
Life	$	$	$
Health	$	$	$
Disability	$	$	$
Income Taxes	$	$	$
Food	$	$	$
Entertainment	$	$	$
Clothing	$	$	$
Child Care	$	$	$
Education	$	$	$
Vacation	$	$	$
Contributions	$	$	$
Alimony/Child Support	$	$	$
Other Payments	$	$	$
TOTAL EXPENSES	$	$	$

CASH FLOW/INCOME COMPARISON

FOR THE MONTH OF: ____________

INCOME	PROJECTED	ACTUAL	(+ OR -)
Salary	$	$	$
Commission	$	$	$
Bonuses	$	$	$
Alimony/Child Support	$	$	$
Interest	$	$	$
Dividends	$	$	$
Rents and Royalties	$	$	$
Partnership Distribution	$	$	$
Pensions	$	$	$
Other INcome	$	$	$
TOTAL CASH AVAILABLE	$	$	$

Assessing Your Cash Flow

Over 75% of American consumers are living from payday to payday with virtually nothing left at the end of the month. After working with hundreds of people, I am convinced there is no level of income one cannot outspend.

Assessing your net inflow indicates whether or not you are living within your means and establishes the amount of net cash available for:

- Savings
- Investments
- Debt Reduction
- Future Goals

Cash flow funds are divided into three categories:

1. Maintaining Funds
   - Rent/Mortgage
   - Utilities
   - Food
   - Etc.

2. Future/Investment Funds
   - Retirement Accounts
   - Savings
   - Investments

3. Deficit Funds
   - Auto Loans
   - Credit Cards
   - Other Debts

The goal is to convert as much maintaining and deficit funds as possible into investment funds. This conversion should be done on a permanent basis and these investment funds should never be used for maintaining funds or deficit funds. There is no need great enough to risk your future wealth.

The majority of finance books for years have given the same old advice:

- Pay yourself first.
- Save 10% of what you make.
- It does not work.. Why?
- Nobody will do it. Why?
- They do not know how to save.

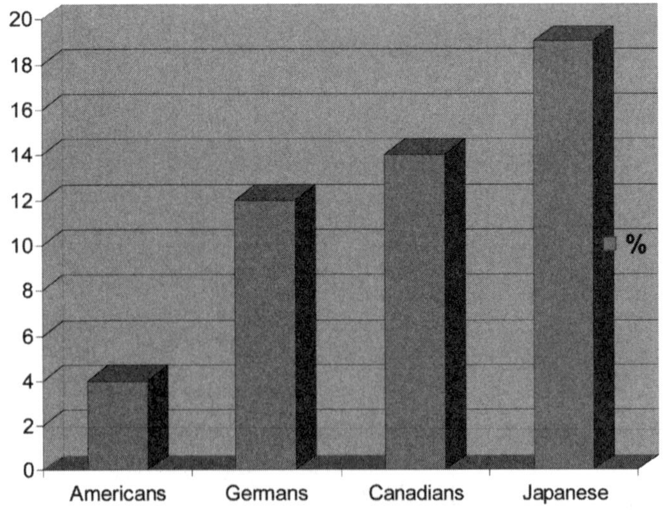

Americans save on average 3%

Germans save on average 12%

Canadians save on average 14%

Japanese save on average 19%

People don't have time to save: they're too busy spending.

—Money Magazine

- How do we convert consumers from a spending mentality to a savings mentality?
- The best place to start is with a tax-deductible retirement plan. This is where you will get the most for your money and withdrawal of these funds would result in a penalty.

BE YOUR OWN ASSET MANAGER

The greatest discovery of my generation is that a human being can alter his life by altering his attitudes of mind.

—William James

The number one reason people fail financially is procrastination. We tell ourselves "I'll do it later" or "I'll have someone else do it." Who could ever care more about your finances than you? No one! Let's consider the following scenario:

You have now been hired to be the CFO (Chief Financial Officer) of a very important asset management firm. But you say "I don't know anything about being a CFO, let alone the field of asset management."

However, in reality, you have held this position for some time. It is your own asset management we are referring to and we want to view it from the position of an outside expert coming in to run it. You are the incoming CFO that will turn this company around and bring new levels of profitability. For this job your compensation and future will be based on your results.

So let us begin with how your company stands currently. Complete the following worksheet with the facts on your personal asset management company.

The Art of Portfolio Construction

Asset Analysis

The purpose of analyzing your current asset portfolio is two-fold. First, you want to determine whether or not your assets are adequately diversified. Second, you want to know how each asset is performing. Assets are divided into two main categories:

1. Working Assets
2. Reserve Assets

Complete the following page to show how you currently stand. The next two pages are used for proposing changes in the current plan and what effects these changes will have.

ASSET ANALYSIS

AS OF ____________________________

WORKING ASSETS	NET VALUE	ANNUAL INCOME	YIELD %	ESTIMATED APPREC.
1. SAVINGS ACCOUNTS				
2. MONEY MARKET				
3. CERTIFICATES OF DEPOSIT				
4. COMMON STOCKS				
5. BONDS				
6. MUTUAL FUNDS				
7. REAL ESTATE (Not including personal residence; current value less mortgage)				
8. ANNUITIES				
9. NOTES RECEIVABLE				
10. BUSINESS INTEREST				
11. OTHER ASSETS				
12. TOTAL WORKING ASSETS				

RESERVE ASSETS	NET VALUE
13. PERSONAL RESIDENCE (Current value less mortgage)	
14. IRA	
15. 401K'S	
16. VESTED INTEREST IN PENSION & PROFIT SHARING	
17. OTHER	
18. TOTAL RESERVE ASSETS	

19. TOTAL WORKING ASSETS (LINE 12)	
20. ANNUAL INCOME (LINE 12)	
21. TOTAL RESERVE ASSETS (LINE 18)	

Proposed Portfolio

WORKING ASSETS	NET VALUE	ANNUAL INCOME	YIELD %	ESTIMATED APPREC.
1. SAVINGS ACCOUNTS				
2. MONEY MARKET				
3. CERTIFICATES OF DEPOSIT				
4. COMMON STOCKS				
5. BONDS				
6. MUTUAL FUNDS				
7. REAL ESTATE (Not including personal residence; current value less mortgage)				
8. ANNUITIES				
9. NOTES RECEIVABLE				
10. BUSINESS INTEREST				
11. OTHER ASSETS				
12. TOTAL WORKING ASSETS				

RESERVE ASSETS				
13. PERSONAL RESIDENCE (Current value less mortgage)				
14. IRA				
15. 401K'S				
16. VESTED INTEREST IN PENSION & PROFIT SHARING				
17. OTHER				
18. TOTAL RESERVE ASSETS				

19. TOTAL WORKING ASSETS (LINE 12)				
20. ANNUAL INCOME (LINE 12)				
21. TOTAL RESERVE ASSETS (LINE 18)				

Comparison Portfolio After Adjustment

	TOTAL	INCOME	YIELD	ESTIMATED APPREC.
1. CURRENT WORING PORTFOLIO				
2. PROPOSED WORKING PORTFOLIO				
3. DOLLAR CHANGE				
4. PERCENTAGE CHANGE				
5. CURRENT RESERVE ASSETS				
6. PROPOSED RESERVE ASSETS				
7. DOLLAR CHANGE				
8. PERCENTAGE CHANGE				

Future Funding Schedule			
One of the major parts of any financial plan includes the setting of future financial objectives. The chart below was designed to be used for this purpose.			
OBJECTIVE	COST	PRIORITY	YEAR TO BE ACCOMPLISHED

PRIORITY

A - A MUST HAVE
B - BETTER HAVE IT
C - COULD TAKE IT OR LEAVE IT
D - DO NOT NEED

There are two times in a man's life when he should not speculate: when he can't afford it, and when he can.

—Mark Twain

Spreading Your Risk

Investments are categorized from safe to speculative, according to the degree of risk involved. The structure used here is that of a building with each tier of investment block carefully laid upon the other. The tiers are set up to build upon a firm foundation or base with each successive tier designed to reinforce the base and add potential for gain. As you move up the financial tiers, you see an ever increasing risk element.

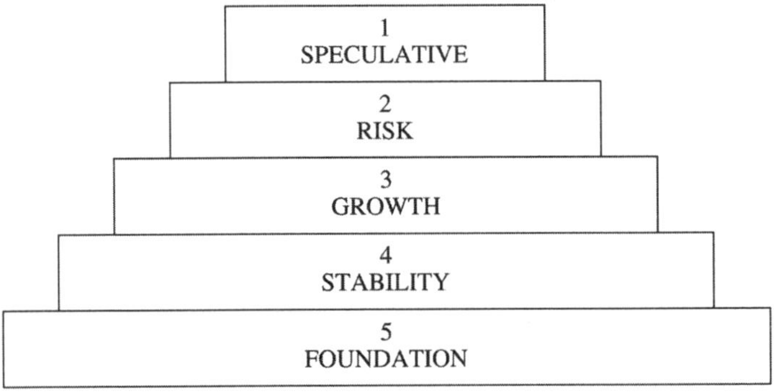

The investment tiered construction reflects the risk-reward characteristics of various types of investments. The Investment Risk Chart has five tiers, with each tier representing different investment levels of risk. The tiers are numbered 1 through 5, 1 being the highest risk and 5 the lowest. The larger the number, the greater amount of assets should be placed in this tier.

Investment Risk Chart

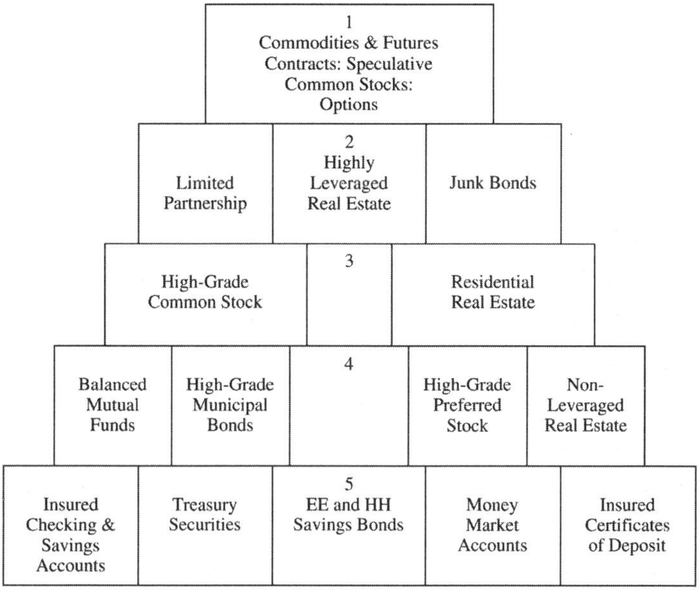

1. High risk; increasing profit potential 2. Medium to high risk
3. & 4. Low to Medium Risk; decreasing profit potential 5. No to Low Risk; sideline money

The Investment Risk Chart illustrates how to construct an ideal investment portfolio. Investments are measured by the financial return they generate. Each investment offers a different level or opportunity of return and each investment carries a different degree of risk. The Investment Risk Chart above ranks investments 1-5 based on risk.

1 & 2 HIGH RISK
3 & 4 MEDIUM RISK
ANYTHING BELOW 4 IS LOW TO NO RISK

INVESTMENT PORTFOLIO ALLOCATION

The plans of the diligent lead to profit
(Proverbs 21:5).

What investments should you choose and in what amounts? The answer to this question is based on the type of investor you are. There are three basic types of investors:

1. Safe
2. Conservative
3. Aggressive

Note: There is one other major category which is not included in the basic investor types: the Sideline Investor. The Sideline Investor is one who would not use the word investor at all. Saver would be the better term. The goal is to save their money invested and to avoid risk at all cost. They are the bystanders in the investment game; they show up, but rarely ever enter the game.

Sideline money is something financial analyst's measure all the time. It is the pulse of consumer sentiment. As sideline money accumulates, the more conservative is the feeling of the average consumer.

Once sideline money starts to enter the investment market place, it is a sign that the average consumer feels strongly about the economy. It is also a signal for the investor to get out of the market. The investment theory is based on the assumption that when the safe investor or the average consumer buys, it is time to sell.

Example: From 1979-1980, gold was rising very quickly. It was on the news every night; "Gold up again today. Gold hits a new high." When gold hit $800 an ounce, the masses moved in to buy. Then gold started back down. Once gold bottomed out, the masses sold. Now, with their new found loss and the gain of an even more safety attitude, they are back to putting all funds in only safe areas.

Again, in 1999-2000, a new investment craze was "in." This time it was the dot.com boom, a time when conservative investors were investing into speculative stocks. I knew several investors who redesigned their retirement accounts from large stocks and bonds to dot.coms. At the time, they were convinced this was a wise investment move. Unlike gold, where investors bought high and sold low, this time they did not have to sell low, many of the companies went under leaving investors with nothing.

Looking at the Investment Risk Chart, gold would be at the very top of the risk and not a place for a first big move in the investment game.

SAFE INVESTOR

This investor has the largest percentage of funds in the no-to-low risk areas with some funds in growth investments.

INVESTMENTS SAFE INVESTOR

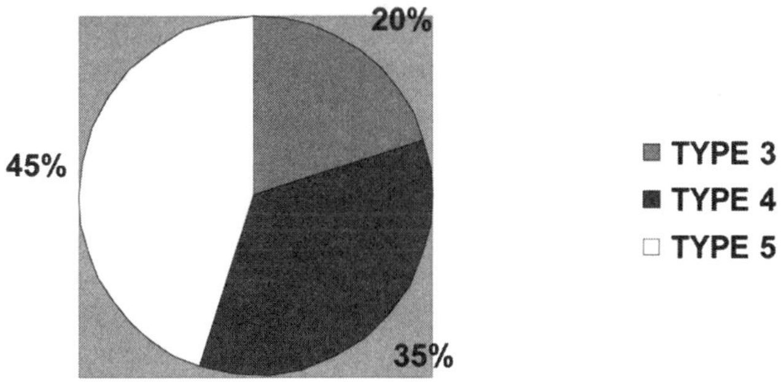

The safe investor has 20% of their investments in category 3, low to medium risk; 35% are in category 4, also low to medium risk; while 45% of their investments are in category 5, no to low risk or sideline money.

INVESTMENTS

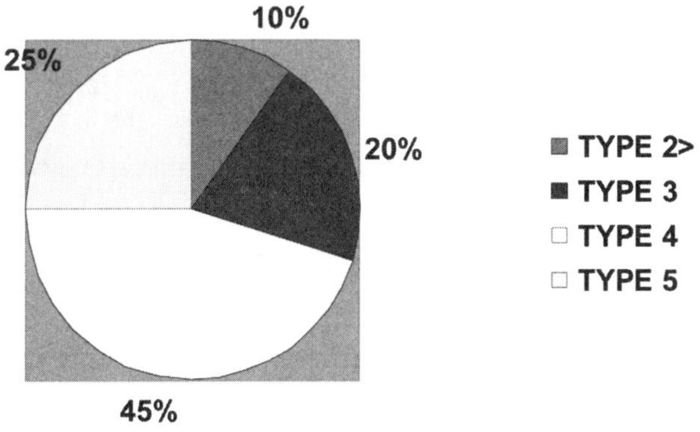

CONSERVATIVE INVESTOR

The Conservative Investor has 10% of their investments in category 2 or higher, medium risk; 20% in category 3, low to medium risk; 25% in category 5, low to no risk, sideline money; and 45% in category 4, also low to medium risk.

INVESTMENTS AGGRESSIVE INVESTOR

The majority of the Aggressive Investor's funds are in greater risk investments. Growth is the goal, using assets working to accumulate greater assets.

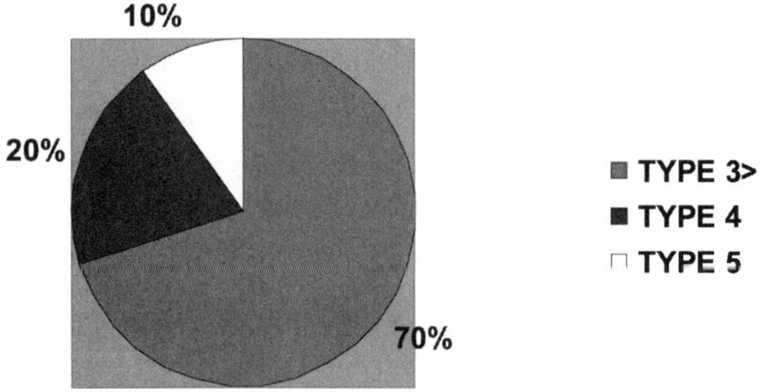

The Aggressive Investor has 70% of their investments in category 3 or higher, low to medium risk; 20% in category 4, also low to medium risk; and 10% in category 5, sideline money.

Risk Tolerance Test

The following questions are designed to help you determine the type of investor you may be:

1. You win $25,000 in the lottery. What would you do?

A. Put it all in savings
B. Pay off debts
C. Buy a new car or other items
D. Invest in real estate or stocks

2. What percentage of your total investment assets are you willing to risk on a single aggressive investment?

A. None
B. Less than 10%
C. 10% - 25%
D. Over 25%

3. Your current stock portfolio fell 25% in one quarter. How would you react?

A. Sell all of it
B. Hold until it comes back up
C. Sell at least 50%
D. Buy more

4. Several lending articles came out recently predicting equities will go down in coming years and that real estate outlook is strong. You would...

A. Keep with current investment strategy
B. Hold position
C. Start reducing equity holdings
D. Sell equities and begin buying real estate

5. Which best describes how you feel about investment?
   A. Very conservative
   B. Conservative
   C. Accept moderate risk
   D. Take greater risk for greater gain

6. What is your reaction to selling an investment at loss?

   A. Makes you sick to lose money
   B. Feel relieved to bail out of it
   C. Your philosophy is to sell the losers and hang onto the winners
   D. Not all investments are winners

7. You time horizon for holding an investment to produce results is...

   A. 10 years plus
   B. 6 - 10 years
   C. 3 - 6 years
   D. Less than 2 years

8. Stable income is important to you and you would be willing to give up a higher return for the more stable income.

   True
   False

9. You can not deal with the ups and downs of the stock market.

   True
   False

SCORING

A. 0 Points
B. 2 Points
C. 3 Points
D. 5 Points
True 1 Point
False 3 Points

Safe Investor	Less than 20 Points
Conservative Investor	20 - 30 Points
Aggressive Investor	30+ Points

Money is something to make bookkeeping convenient.
—H.L. Hunt

Understanding Investment Risk

An investor can either accept risk of an investment or choose one of the following:

Risk Avoidance

Investment planning is almost impossible without a thorough understanding of risk. There is a risk/return trade-off. That is, the greater risk accepted, the greater must be the potential return as reward for committing one's funds to an uncertain outcome. Generally, as the level of risk rises the rate of return should also rise and vice versa. One way to handle risk is to avoid it. Risk avoidance occurs when one chooses to completely avoid the activity the risk is associated with.

Risk Transfer

Another way to handle risk is to transfer the risk. An easy to understand example of risk transfer is the concept of insurance. If one has the risk of becoming severely ill (and unfortunately we all do), then health insurance is advisable. An insurance company will allow you to transfer the risk of large medical bills to them in exchange for a fee called an insurance premium.

The Risk Adverse Investor

Do investors dislike risk? In economics in general and investments in particular, the standard assumption is that investors are rational. Rational investors prefer certainty to uncertainty. It is easy to say that investors dislike risk but more precisely, we should say that investors are risk adverse. A risk-adverse investor is one who will not assume risk simply for the sake of risk and will not incur any given level of risk unless there is an expectation of adequate compensation for having done so. Note carefully, it is not irrational to assume risk, even very large risk, as long as we expect to be compensated for it. In fact, investors cannot reasonably expect to earn larger returns without assuming larger risks.

LIFE CYCLE ASSET ALLOCATION

There are dreamers and there are planners; the planners make their dreams come true.

—Edwin Cole

Regardless of your age, income, or amount of assets you have, there will come a time when you will need your assets to be producing greater assets. Many investors produce more assets by "market timing," that is, by moving their assets from one investment vehicle to another according to a program which catches the highs and avoids the lows. The problem with this is—it doesn't work.

There is an alternative program called "asset allocation" that offers a basic foundation to investment management. Age or time is an important

ASSET ALLOCATIONLIFE CYCLE CHART		
AGE	GROWTH (%)	FOUNDATION (%)
25-44	80	20
45-54	70	30
55-64	60	40
65-70	40	60
71 AND OVER	25	75

investment component, but it is one most people- fail to take advantage of.

Age is one important component that investors must consider. Too many young investors do not take advantage of age and utilizing growth assets. Many stick with a very conservative philosophy until later in life when they figure they must play catch up.

Take higher risks at the early stages of life. If we do not plan and put the plan in action today, inevitably we will panic and try to play catch up tomorrow. The greatest asset you have right now is not money - it is time.

Getting Started

Ages 25-44

These are the asset building years. This is a period with a long-term horizon to retirement and should be handled with looking toward the aggressive side. The leading problem with this age category is that it is a hard time to save, but it is also the most critical time to start an investment program. This is the time in which time is on your side. By investing early, you are taking advantage of long-term compounding. Your early years are key and the small choices you make now can have a profound effect on your later life. Whatever seemingly insignificant sums you can put away these days have plenty of time to grow into a significant nest egg. Unfortunately, many people do not take full advantage of this time. Less than a third of workers in their twenties and thirties max out their 401(k) plans - which means they may be missing out on some company matching, a benefit that is basically free money.

Steps to Do Now

1. Pay off all your credit card debt and student loans as soon as possible. The compounding effect of interest is a true wealth killer.

2. Max out your 401(k) plan.

3. Establish and fund maximum to a Roth IRA.

4. Allocate your 401(k) and your IRA toward growth only investments. Prime Time—Make the Most of Your Earning and Saving Years.

Ages 45-54

During these years, capital growth is the main concern. At this stage, you are reducing your risk category by 5% in order to conserve principal. The majority of assets are still 75% in growth with 25% in safety. During these years, people become greater savers than at any previous time. This is the time of personal and financial maturity, where an investor needs to be actively concerned with his portfolio management. Fortunately, you still have a good 15 to 20 years to continue to be an aggressive investor. The traditional rule of thumb - that in retirement you will need 70% of what you make now - may be an outdated assumption. Examine this area very closely.

Steps to Do Now

1. Continue to contribute the maximum to your 401(k) and IRA accounts.

2. Review retirement goals. How much, in today's dollars would you ideally like to have annually after retirement?

3. It is not too early to begin estate planning.

Home Stretch – Fine Tune Your Goals and Strategies

Ages 55-64

During this stage, your income will be at its maximum and should be in full cycle for retirement funding. Growth investments should be reduced by 10% to 65%. This is a time to apportion portfolios away from aggressive to moderate growth. Investments should be toward capital accumulation that provides a predictable lump sum which can be converted to retirement income. At what age will you ultimately retire? Will any children still be in college? Do you expect your parents to need support?

Steps to Do Now

1. A full estate plan should be in place.

2. Review how your assets are allocated.

3. Begin to reduce mortgage on your home.

You Passed Go – Is It Time To Collect?

Age 65 and over

The majority of individuals of this stage become overly conservative. There should still be 40% in growth assets, this is a 20% decrease of placement of assets in the growth categories. The objective of this portfolio is maximum capital preservation. While maintaining principal is the key, you must also protect against the effects of inflation with some growth investments. Here, formerly appropriate investments no longer fit current needs. Now it's time to take stock, ponder some lifestyle choices and maybe make some trade-offs. Will you work part-time? Will you move or downsize? Are you in good health?

Steps to Do Now

1. Check on Social Security benefits (www.ssa.gov) or call 1-800-772-1213.

2. Look at rollover strategies for your 401(k) or other company retirement plans.

3. Review your estate plan with your financial advisor or estate attorney.

In summary, the different stages of the life cycle place emphasis on different parts of the investment portfolio. Each part is important, but each attains greater importance at progressing stages of the life cycle.

Example: $1,000 invested annually would have the following results:

END OF YEAR	AMOUNT SAVED	5%	10%	15%
5	$5,000	$5,802	$6,716	$7,754
10	$10,000	$13,207	$17,531	$23,345
15	$15,000	$22,657	$34,950	$54,717
20	$20,000	$34,719	$63,002	$117,810

Antonio: *Age is like a fine wine.*
Joe: *Yeah, it gets better with age.*
Antonio: *Up until a point, then it sours and every thing settles to the bottom and they can't get rid of you fast enough.*

—Wings

RETIREMENT

If you only knock long enough and loud enough at the gate, you are sure to wake up somebody.
—Henry Wadsworth Longfellow

Most people do not have sufficient money for retirement. Social Security Administration did a study which produced the following results:

- 1.5% were wealthy
- 5.5% were secure
- 4% had to keep working to support themselves
- 89% were dependent on charity, relatives, or friends for their survival

Retired and Still Working

Last year, there were more people 55 and older in the work force than at any time since the U.S. Bureau of

Labor Statistics began publishing the date in 1948. This is just the beginning of what is expected to be an older worker onslaught that will reshape the face of working America.

The bureau projects between 2005 and 2015, the annual growth rate in the job market of the 55 and older group will be four times the annual growth rate for the overall labor force. By 2015, nearly one in four American workers will be 55 or older. The growth in the labor force participation rate stands out significantly among all age categories. What the statistics do not tell us about this increase is if the older workers are being forced back to work or not retiring because of economics, health-care costs, or because they want to work.

Economists note that most Americans have done a poor job of saving for retirement. Some studies show the typical household savings rate is as low as 1 percent of income. Thus, many retirees are finding they can not maintain their lifestyles on Social Security alone. AARP recently reported 68 percent of workers between the ages of 50 and 70 plans to work in retirement or never retire.

The definition of retirement is changing. The baby boom generation–those born between 1946 and 1964 is 77 million strong. Many of this generation are not planning to move to a beach resort area and be satisfied with playing golf. The boomer dream for many is to continue working, but without as much stress. They want a blend of satisfying work and enjoyment. For some the reality holds no option but to keep working. For others, the plan is to give back to society by volunteering time to causes they feel driven to help. The longer money in the form of income keeps coming in, the less you will need from your savings. Working just three years longer can reduce the amount of assets needed to finance retirement by 20%.

What Are Your Retirement Goals?

Remember as a child people asking you, "What do you want to be when you grow up?" The question was not about you, it was an adult looking for advice. What is your goal for retirement? You have three choices:

1. To Survive
2. To be Secure
3. To be Financially Independent

Why is it when I ask this question in our seminars no one chooses to survive and most want to be financially independent? But statistics show survival is what most people end up doing, and that is tragic. A little planning is the difference between simply surviving or being secure. Planning is more than just thinking about it, it requires application. The statistics verify that most people have a plan to keep working all their lives and retire poor. If it is not their plan then they just were very poor at implementing the plan they had. According to the U.S. Department of Health, Education and Welfare at age 65:

70% of those living were dependent on the

government or family

10% were still working because they must

10% were financially independent

Looking at these statistics, the question is, when you are at retirement age, which group do you plan to be in? I know which one you want to be in. Let me ask you again, "Where do you want to be at retirement?" So why is it 90% fail to have their plans work out?

How to Retire with $1,000,000

Assuming a 12% annual return, the following monthly investment would be needed to reach $1,000,000.

AGE	MONTHLY INVESTMENT	VALUE AT AGE 65
25	$104	$1,000,000
35	$328	$1,000,000
40	$594	$1,000,000
50	$2,121	$1,000,000

Think of it: $1,000,000 by only saving $104 a month.

So, you are saying you are 40 years old and there is no way you can afford $594 a month. Then start with less. Just start with something. At $150 a month, you would accumulate over $250,000 by age 65.

WARNING! SOCIAL SECURITY WILL NOT BE ENOUGH!

When social security began, each pensioner was supported by fifty tax-paying workers. By 1960, the ratio was 16 to 1. In 1990, it was 4 to 1 and by the year 2015, it will stand at 2 to 1. As the baby boomers retire, this ratio will fall. The other problem comes from life expectancy. In 1935, when social security was set up the life expectancy of a 65 year old was 12.5 years, today it is 17.5 years. That is a 40% increase the social security benefits must pay out.

There are two basic solutions to this problem:

1. More taxes

2. Raise the retirement age

You can get a projection of your social security benefits from the agency's web site: www.saa.gov. For example, a 60 year old earning $50,000 would receive a monthly benefit of $1,350, and a 60 year old earning $100,000 would receive a monthly benefit of $1,900.

Reaching Financial Independence	
HOW MUCH DO YOU NEED FOR RETIREMENT?	
1. ANNUAL INCOME YOU WILL NEED IN TODAY'S DOLLARS	
2. NUMBER OF YEARS UNTIL RETIREMENT	
3. CAPITALIZATION FACTOR	
4. TOTAL AMOUNT NEEDED	
5. ESTMIATED ANNUAL PENSION	
6. ESTIMATED SOCIAL SECURITY (See Table Below, Multiply by Factor in Column A)	
7. SUBTRACT THE TOTAL OF LINE 5 AND 6 FROM LINE 4	
8. CURRENT TOTAL OF SAVINGS AND INVESTMENTS	
9. CAPITALIZATION FACTOR FROM COLUMN B	
10. WHAT YOUR SAVINGS WILL GROW TO BY THE TIME YOU RETIRE (Line 8 times Line 9)	
11. TOTAL ADDITIONAL SAVINGS YOU WILL NEED (Line 7 minus Line 10)	
12. AMOUNT YOU WILL NEED TO SAVE EACH YEAR (Select Factor from Column C Capitalization. Take that Factor times Line 11.)	

NUMBER OF YEARS	COLUMN A	COLUMN B	COLUMN C
1	1.04	1.09	1.00
2	1.08	1.18	.490
3	1.12	1.29	.320
4	1.17	1.41	.235
5	1.22	1.53	.185
6	1.27	1.67	.151
7	1.32	1.82	.127
8	1.37	1.99	.109
9	1.42	2.17	.095
10	1.48	2.36	.083
15	1.80	3.64	.050
20	2.19	5.60	.034
25	2.67	8.62	.024

SELECTING A FINANCIAL ADVISOR

If a plan is the road to your financial dreams, then your planner is the key to the car. —J.C.

Looking for a title? Is it financial planner, financial consultant, or financial advisor? What is in a name? The title is of little value today because life insurance agents, stockbrokers, mutual funds salespeople, bankers, mortgage bankers, accountants, etc., may be using the title financial planner-consultant-advisor. What really matters is the individual with whom you do business.

Things to consider when choosing a financial person:

How do you pay for their services? Where does their compensation come from? Is it based on fees, sales commissions, or a combination? Fee-only financial advice is theoretically an unbiased person.

This should be very important. The negative point most commission-based financial planners bring up, is the fee-only planner does not have the motivation to help you implement the plan.

They believe people will not follow or do anything with the plan. That is like saying "accountants will do your tax return for a fee, but since they are not paid on a percentage, there would be no motivation to mail in the return." Give me a break! Oh sure, the IRS provides the motivation, you are thinking.

All right, you go in to an attorney because you are in over your head financially and the advice is to file bankruptcy. Your attorney tells you it will cost $750 up-front for the service. You pay with the last bit of money you have. You are told to go home and get a complete list of all your creditors and how much you owe. Once you do they will file the papers. You go home and forget what the attorney told you. I do not think so. Most people who pay for advice usually follow it.

Be aware the commission-only financial salesperson may have a possible conflict of interest. The conflict of interest is who's financial well-being are they most concerned with? Remember, in the real world there is the possibility of a conflict of interest in just about every transaction that involves your money.

Other considerations:

- What is the person's success "track" record?

- Do they provide you with numerous

references so you can find out others experience?

- What is their knowledge base or capabilities? Their knowledge base should not be limited to only a few areas, but on the other hand you want them to tell you where their expertise stops. A professional financial person will work with other professionals from accounting, legal, or whatever expertise is needed.

- Is their plan to develop an overall financial strategy for you? The advice or plan should be based on your financial goals and risk tolerance. If your advisor does not spend a good deal of time examining your objectives and attitude, then shop for a new one. A financial planner must be sensitive and responsive to your attitudes and objectives.

Financial planning is an evolutionary process. Periodic evaluations and reviews are necessary. Consequently, the relationship with your advisor should be a continuing one as long as you are properly and competently advised.

List of Advisors

AS OF: ______________________

ATTORNEY:	
NAME OF FIRM:	
ADDRESS OF FIRM:	
TELEPHONE NUMBER:	
DOCUMENTS ON FILE WITH ATTY:	
ACCOUNTANT/TAX ADVISOR:	
NAME OF FIRM:	
ADDRESS OF FIRM:	
TELEPHONE NUMBER:	
DOCUMENTS ON FILE:	
PERSONAL BANKER:	
NAME OF BANK:	
ADDRESS OF BANK:	
TELEPHONE NUMBER:	
INVESTMENT BANKER:	
NAME OF FIRM:	
ADDRESS OF FIRM:	
TELEPHONE NUMBER:	
ACCOUNT NUMBER:	
ACCOUNT NUMBER:	
SECURITIES HELD WITH BANKER:	
FINANCIAL PLANNER:	
NAME OF FIRM:	
ADDRESS OF FIRM:	
TELEPHONE NUMBER:	
INFORMATION OF FILE:	
INSURANCE AGENTS	

LIFE INSURANCE AGENT:	
NAME OF INSURANCE COMPANY:	
ADDRESS:	
TELEPHONE NUMBER:	
POLICY NUMBERS:	
HEALTH INSURANCE AGENT:	
NAME OF INSURANCE COMPANY:	
ADDRESS:	
TELEPHONE NUMBER:	
POLICY NUMBERS/INFORMATION:	
AUTO/HOME INSURANCE AGENT:	
NAME OF INSURANCE COMPANY:	
ADDRESS:	
TELEPHONE NUMBER:	
POLICY NUMBERS/INFORMATION:	

Interview Questions for Perspective Advisors
NAME:
1. What is their area of specialty?
2. What is their educational background?
3. Do they hold any professional designations?
4. How long have they been in practice?
5. How long have they been with their present firm?
6. What is their fee structure?
7. With whom will I be working?
8. Who handles business if your advisor is unavailable?
9. Do they consult with other professionals?
10. How much will it cost?

Advisor Evaluation		
NAME OF ADVISOR:		
DATE OF INTERVIEW:		
RATING SYSTEM (1) UNSATISFACTORY TO (5) EXCELLENT		
EVALUATION AREA	RATING	COMMENTS
EDUCATIONAL BACKGROUND		
EXPERIENCE		
FEE STRUCTURE		
ATTITUDE AND ABILITY TO RELATE TO ME PERSONALLY		
CONVENIENCE OF OFFICE		
TOTAL NUMBER OF POINTS:		
ADDITIONAL COMMENTS:		

THE PROSPERITY MODEL

Do not go where the path may lead, go instead where there is no path and leave a trail.

—Ralph Waldo Emerson

It is absolutely essential that you begin to think prosperous thoughts if your desire is to be financially secure. A positive focus on prosperity can be difficult, when the reality of your every day life is everything but prosperous. You see, prosperity must first be in your mind before it can be achieved. Increasing your ability to build wealth is more than just knowing what kind of investments to make. It is more than just becoming financially literate. First it involves the overcoming of one's skepticism about wealth. Too many people have an attitude full of doubt when it comes to prosperity or wealth building. They find it much easier to talk about how financial security can not be done rather than to work toward the accomplishment of prosperity.

> *All hard work brings a profit, but mere talk leads only to poverty. The wealth of the wise is their crown, but the folly of fools yields folly (*Proverbs 14: 23-24).

The point in these two verses is mere talk will not do it, you need to work a proven plan, and avoid costly unprofitable actions.

> *He who works his land will have abundant food, but the one who chases fantasies will have his fill of poverty (*Proverbs 28:19).

This verse warns against giving up on work and trying to shortcut the system with an idea of "get rich quick." Avoid that which promises high returns for little or nothing invested, be it time or money.

There is an old fable about the Devil offering to sell some tools of his trade. For sale were tools such as the dagger of deceit and the hammer of hatred. One of the priciest tools in his bag of evil was a harmless looking wedge. When questioned as to why a simple wedge was carrying such a high price, the Devil answered, "This harmless looking wedge is far from any simple tool, it is in fact my most powerful and dependable weapon in my arsenal. I call it the wedge of doubt. I know I can always count on doubt and discouragement to destroy the will of man and have him give up all hope."

The moral of the fable is quite simple; the power of doubt can keep you from ever reaching your goals. Once doubt wedges in, you begin to question your plans and your abilities to complete them.

Financial prosperity becomes a dismissed venture, replaced by fears and doubt.

> *Invest in truth and wisdom, discipline, and good sense, and do not part with them (*Proverbs 23:23 CEV).

Your doubt and fears are not the only stumbling blocks stopping you. Your friends and family enjoy sharing their fears, doubts, failures, and reasons why you can not succeed.

> *Words of wisdom come from the wise, but fools speak foolishness (*Proverbs 15:2 CEV).

> *Words of wisdom make good sense; the thoughts of a fool make no sense at all* (Proverbs 15:7 CEV).

> *Fools have no desire to learn; they would much rather give their own opinion (*Proverbs 18:2 CEV).

Proverbs is very clear on the point "talk is cheap." Words can build people up or tear them down. Kind words are good medicine. As parents, brothers, sisters, or friends we must encourage others and refrain from expressing any negative thoughts.

There are several reasons keeping you from becoming prosperous:

8 Reasons Why People Do Not Become Prosperous

There is a real science to becoming prosperous. Like math or engineering, there are a precise set of laws which govern the process of acquiring wealth, and once learned and followed anyone can become prosperous with a mathematical certainty. After years of working with multi-millionaires and teaching the system to others, it proves the application of these principles creates wealth. Those who fail to become prosperous do not know or apply these principles. They assume prosperity is something based more on luck or high risk. Nothing could be further from reality. I will introduce you to a proven system of acquiring wealth, but first you need to know the reasons why people do not obtain prosperity.

1. They do not believe it can be done or do not believe *they* can obtain prosperity. You can only achieve what you believe.

2. They have no system or plan to follow. They need to find a system and build a network by finding a mentor (someone who has success at doing it—not just telling you about the system).

3. Wealth becomes a moving target they chase, instead of a precise path to follow.

4. Our education system fails us financially. Personal finance is an elective, if at all, and it teaches you about a checking account and gives you definitions of financial terms. It does not suggest or recommend a thing. You are left knowing the meaning of a

financial term but no idea what to do with the knowledge.

5. Fail to start. It goes beyond procrastination. Over the years in teaching I have seen people who want to continue studying until they know everything. One couple attended one of my seminars four years ago. I ran into them at a recent seminar where I was speaking and found they had yet to start and were still studying. You have to act!

6. Letting others control your finances. You can not delegate the acquisition of wealth to someone who does not have a proven system. You can always plug others into your proven system, but you should never give up control.

7. Not having checks and balances. You need to run your finances as a business. We have included financial forms to assist you. Start with the net worth test.

8. Do not let others pull you down or abandon your plan. We all know those who carry negativity, or are extremely pessimistic. Do not judge them or let them judge your plans to improve yourself.

Calculating Prosperity

Financial prosperity is the ability to support you and your family to live well without working for a living. You have the opportunity to live a life of your own choosing, to have the benefit of leisure time and personal freedom, and not be controlled by the need of a job.

When will I achieve real financial freedom? I have a ratio called the prosperity ratio. Before calculating the prosperity ratio, you must first know the parts making up the ratio. All income from sources other than earned income is the basis of the formula. The key is to have your income outside of work cover your expenses. You see, money comes in the form of income to you in three ways:

Earned Income - Income from working

Passive Income - Income from real estate (rental)

Portfolio Income - Income from interest and dividends on investments

My preference is for passive income. Why? Passive income is usually the least taxed and most likely to increase. Take for example a rental property having a monthly income of $1,000. Do you pay taxes on this full amount? No. The income is offset by any expenses and depreciation. Do rents usually go down? No. Is there a possibility of the asset increasing in value? Yes.

On the other hand, we have my least favorite money source—earned income. It is not because I do not enjoy my work, I do. It is the effect taxes take on the income from working monies. My earned income takes the most time and effort to acquire and I net the least compared to passive or portfolio income.

$$\text{Prosperity Ratio} = \frac{\text{Total passive income–portfolio income}}{\text{Total Expenses}}$$

If your passive income is $1,800 a month, your portfolio income is $500 and your total expenses are $4,000 a month, where are you on the prosperity ratio?

$$\frac{\$1{,}800 + \$500}{\$4{,}000} = \frac{\$2{,}300}{\$4{,}000} = .58$$

You are 58% of the way there. Your passive and portfolio income needs to increase by 42% or $1,700 a month. Once the prosperity ratio equals 1 or 100% of your total expenses, you are at financial freedom and are free to walk away from your job.

$$\frac{\text{Passive income + Portfolio income}}{\text{Total Expenses}} = \frac{3{,}000 + 1{,}000}{4{,}000} = 1.00$$

Calculate your prosperity ratio. List your monthly incomes below:

Earned Income $ ________________ monthly

Passive Income $ ________________ monthly

Portfolio Income $ ________________ monthly

Add up your total monthly expenses.

$$\frac{\text{Passive Income + Portfolio Income}}{\text{Total Expenses}} = \text{(your answer)}$$

What is your prosperity ratio and what percentage do you need to reach financial freedom? Do you have a long way to go? Do not worry, the final section of this book is going to introduce you to a proven method of acquiring passive income sufficient to achieve financial freedom. Let us take another look at the definition of prosperity in relation to financial freedom. Financial prosperity is: The amount of time you can maintain your standard of living without working.

If your prosperity ratio is .75 you take the 25% shortage and divide it by your assets to determine the amount of time you can maintain your standard of living. Using the monthly expenses of $4,000 a month and 75% coming in the form of passive and portfolio income of $3,000, the shortage is $1,000 a month. At the rate of reducing your investments and savings by $1,000 a month, how long will it last? Not fun is it? Most do not look at this until they are retired and must then focus on reducing their life style or continue to work. This is something that can and should be avoided.

Prosperity Profit Plan: Wealth Accumulation Made Simple

There are numerous ways to build wealth today. Many require years of training, and others require a good base of money or assets to begin, and still others employ a higher degree of risk. I would like to focus on a proven plan of building wealth. This is a good place to begin your accumulation process, but by no way the end of your journey.

My basic recommendation to anyone starting out on their wealth building is to start with the following:

1. Maximum annual contribution to your 401K.

2. Maximum annual contribution to a Roth IRA.

3. Buy under valued rental property, improve it, rent it, and hold it.

4. Do not touch any of the above until your desired prosperity ratio is achieved.

The 401K is absolutely something you must do for those working at a company offering the program. I am constantly amazed at those who do not make the maximum contribution when their company offers to match the contribution. When asked, the response is usually the same–retirement is so far away. Ask a different question, "How many of you would invest the maximum you could if you were guaranteed 50% on your money?" More people seem to have "buy in" to this approach.

$ 1,000	Invested in Your 401K
$ 250	Employer Contribution
$ 280	Tax Benefit

This is 53% on your money if you earned 0% growth. People are searching for the next hot stock or the latest fad to invest their money. Stop searching, and maximize the plain, simple, and safer 401K. If the 401K is not available to you, go to the IRA (individual retirement account).

The Roth IRA began in 1998. It is different from the traditional IRA, where the principal invested is tax-deductible in the tax year it is contributed. The funds placed in the Roth IRA are not tax deductible, but all accumulation grows tax-free and will remain tax-free upon withdrawal. This is a substantial wealth difference in the future when the funds are most needed.

Another bonus of the Roth IRA has to do with the distribution rules. With the traditional IRA there is a mandatory withdrawal beginning at age 70, and at the time the money is withdrawn, subject to taxes. Not so with the Roth IRA. You can continue to have your money grow tax-free, and if you still have earned income, you can continue additional contributions.

The advantage of tax-free growth along with tax-free withdraws are so strong financially it may make sense to convert part or all of your traditional IRA to a Roth. Note: the conversion will be taxable, and you can convert any amount you wish or spread it out over time. (Consult your tax advisor on what fits your needs).

The plan is simple, it is low risk, and it works. The problem comes when people are playing catch up, they think they need to complicate things to achieve greater results. When Robert Kiyosaki, author of *Rich Dad Poor Dad* was asked where he learned his formula for getting rich, he replied "Playing the game of MONOPOLY® as a kid. The formula for getting rich in MONOPOLY® is simple, and it works in real life as well as in the game." It is true, becoming prosperous is not rocket science, it can be reached by following a simple plan of accumulating assets. One of the best and proven methods of wealth building is acquiring a single family property under valued, improve it, rent it, and let your tenant's pay off your property. At the time you acquire an under valued property, your net worth has increased. Once rented, your cash flow has increased. The beauty of real estate is you can acquire it for less than market value. Real estate offers benefits other investments cannot produce, making it your ACE wealth accumulator.

Appreciation
Cash Flow
Equity build up – amortization

There are numerous investment opportunities available to you. However, I recommend you focus on only two as you begin.

1. Pre-hab
2. Repair and Rent

The Pre-hab has been my bread and butter cash flow generator. Pre-hab stands for preliminary rehab. It involves fixing the *fear factor* issues. Those are the areas most likely to scare off the inexperienced buyer.

By removing the scare factor your return would be greatly increased. The turn around time is usually shorter than any of the other strategies.

By focusing on only a small number of key improvements, I estimate the return is 3-4 times your money spent on such improvements.

Let us take a look at an example of a pre-hab property I acquired:

Purchase price	$ 99,000
Estimated total repairs needed	$ 70,000
Estimated value after repairs	$275,000

Choice:

1. Invest $70,000 more and up to six months of work

2. Pre-hab and sell

I know what you are thinking, $100,000 gross profit. After real estate commission and closing costs the profit would be closer to $75,000 - $80,000. Is that 3-4 times your $70,000 for improvements? No. By focusing on key improvements, I invested a total of $10,800 more, for a total of $109,800. The property was sold for $178,000, netting $65,000, less commissions and closing costs.

Again, I recommend pre-hab over a complete rehab because it is faster return with less money spent. The second reason is I have seen too many inexperienced people over improve a property or get over charged by their contractor. I have been there – done that! If you do not have the construction knowledge, contacts, or time, avoid this area until you gain the experience.

Repair and Rent is the best strategy for building long term wealth. I recently was one of several seminar speakers at a real estate wealth building boot camp. One evening a couple of other seminar speakers and I were having dinner and one thing they both agreed with was the low tech concept of buying and holding rental property remains the best wealth accumulation method. The only downside for them is it does not sell seminars. People are attached to the next get-rich quick or get rich with less work idea.

> *Dishonest money dwindles away but he who gathers money little by little makes it grow* (Proverbs 13: 11).

Let us look at an example of a repair and rent property:

Purchase price	$ 31,000
Estimated repairs needed	7,000
Total investment	$ 38,000
Estimated value after repairs	$ 70,000

After the repairs were made, the property was rented for $675.00 a month.

$38,000 Loan at 7% interest	=	$ 225.84 monthly
Taxes and Insurance	=	$ 150.16 per month
Total Payment	=	$ 376.00 per month
Net cash flow	=	$ 299.00 a month

Several months later, an investor offered $50,000 for the house, which would net an $11,000 profit. What would you do? Collect the $ 299.00 profit a month or take $ 11,000 profit now? It would take 36 months of $ 299.00 to equal the $ 11,000. You are thinking, take the $ 11,000 in profit and acquire another property. Is there another option beyond sell or hold? Since the property has been owned for one year, the opportunity of refinancing and taking cash out is available. Most lenders do not allow cash out refinancing until the property has been owned for a minimum of 12 months. The property was appraised at $74,000. The new loan would be $59,200 at 6.25% interest with a payment of $364.50, plus taxes and insurance. Let us compare our choices:

Option 1 - Net rental income $ 299.00 per month

Option 2 - Sell for $ 11,000 profit

Option 3 - Refinance, pull cash out of $21,200, plus continue to net $ 187.00 per month in rental income.

Option 3 of course, is the best choice and it gets better. Option 2 would have a gross income of

$11,000 and it would be subject to income taxes on the long-term gain. However, option 3 nets $21,200 with no tax (the property was not sold).

When most think of a buy and hold strategy, they fail to realize there are opportunities within the hold strategy to free up funds for further investing. When you first review the typical buy and hold plan., it seems it would take forever for your investments to add up to anything, especially if focus is only on net income of a few hundred dollars a month.

So let us enhance our plan. Instead of buying and holding every property, we will establish a yearly set formula. For example, we will buy and hold 50% of our properties and sell the other 50% in year one. The properties are all under valued houses with some need of improvement. The decision is what repair work should you do. Most real estate gurus are advocating flipping the property immediately for a quick pay day. That is certainly an option, but usually not the most profitable.

The path to prosperity is a process. There are numerous roads you can travel and many different investment vehicles you can use along your journey. The investment concepts highlighted briefly in this book are proven to be safe, simple, and successful tools used by myself and many others. This is by no means an all conclusive approach.

Closing Thoughts

In closing, my hope is this book will help you take control of your credit and finances. Knowledge can put you on the path to a more prosperous life. Take what you have learned, put it into action. Not only will you prosper financially, but at the same time you will improve your life and the opportunity to help those around you. If you will trust in God and do what He wants with the gifts given you, God's abundance will flow into your life.

Yours in prosperity and friendship,

Jerry

Glossary

Adjustable Rate Mortgage (ARM) – A floating or fluctuating loan rate that adjusts periodically.

Annual Percentage Rate (APR) - The actual rate consumers pay on a loan expressed as simple interest.

Arrears - A general term used to describe any loan payment or debt that is past due. It's most often used to describe back-owed child support.

Assets - Financial assets are items of value.

Automatic Stay - An injunction, or court order, that takes effect when a bankruptcy petition is filed. An automatic stay prohibits all collection action against a debtor.

Avoidance Powers - The powers used by a trustee to reverse transfers of the debtor's property.

Balance Sheet - A statement of financial conditions as of a specific date. It is different from a cash flow statement, which summarizes income and expenses.

Balloon Payment - A final lump sum payment on an installment contract, such as a mortgage or car loan, which is larger than earlier payments.

Bankruptcy - A legal proceeding in which you are

relieved from paying your debts. There are two kinds of bankruptcies for individuals, Chapter 7 and Chapter 13. In Chapter 7 bankruptcy, you may be required to give up some property in exchange for the erasure of your debts. In Chapter 13 bankruptcy, you don't have to give up any property, but you must pay off a portion of your debts over three to five years. At the end of the three-to-five-year period, the balance of what you owe is wiped out.

Bankruptcy Code - The body of a federal statutory law that governs the bankruptcy process.

Bankruptcy Petition - The legal instrument filed with the bankruptcy court that commences a bankruptcy proceeding.

Basis Point - One basis point equals .01 percent. If the average mortgage rate rise 10 basis point, that would translate into an increase from, say, 8.5 to 8.6 percent.

Biweekly Mortgage - A form of prepayment. Pay one-half of mortgage payment every two weeks, thus making 26 payments a year.

Bond - A debt obligation issued by a corporation or a federal, state, or local government. A bond is evidence of debt on which the issuing corporation or government promises to pay a specific amount of interest for a specified length of time.

Cash Flow - Amount of money one has coming in

and how much is going out.

Capital Gains – Profit realized on the sale or exchange of a capital asset.

Certificate of Deposit – A time deposit investment issued by banks. The time certificate of deposit is characterized by its set of maturity and interest rate.

Chapter 7 – In a Chapter 7 proceeding, the debtor's business is liquidated and its assets are distributed to creditors with allowed proofs of claims.

Chapter 11 – Chapter 11 is a reorganization proceeding. The debtor continues to operate its business after the bankruptcy is filed. Chapter 11 liquidations are commonplace and usually result from an unsuccessful reorganization attempt.

Chapter 13 – Chapter 13 may only be filed by an individual debtor with limited debt. In essence, it allows a payment plan for an individual's financial and / or business debts.

Collateral – Property pledged as security for repayment of a secured debt.

Complaint – A pleading that is filed to initiate a lawsuit or an adversary proceeding.

Compounding – The payment of interest on interest, which is added to the principal with interest then paid on the larger amount.

Consumer Credit - Short-term loans to individuals for the purchase of consumer goods and services.

Consumer Credit Counseling Services - These are non-profit organizations established to help debtors make payment arrangements with creditors.

Credit Bureau - An establishment in the business of collecting information relating to credit and providing credit reports to merchants for a fee.

Credit Rating - The point system used by a credit bureau to indicate a person's payment history.

Credit Report - This report contains information from a credit bureau giving a credit rating and financial data concerning a person or business.

Creditor - One to whom you own money.

Debtor - One who owes debts. In bankruptcy, the bankrupt business that is under the control and protection of the bankruptcy court is the debtor.

Debtor-In-Possession (DIP) - The business debtor in Chapter 11 reorganization. In a Chapter 11, this is the debtor retaining possession of the assets involved in the bankruptcy.

Default Judgment - If you are sued and you do not file papers in response to the lawsuit within the time allowed, the plaintiff (the person who sued you) can ask the court to enter a default judgment against you. When a default judgment is entered, you have lost the case. You can try to get the default judgment set aside, but it can be difficult to do so.

Deficiency Judgment - The difference between the amount you owe a creditor who has foreclosed on your house or repossesses an item of personal property, and the amount that the sale of the property brings in. A deficiency judgment is different from a court judgment in several ways. First, in most states, the creditor does not have to sue you to get a deficiency judgment. He gets it automatically after selling your property. Second, although the creditor can write or call demanding payment, he cannot attach your wages or place a lien on your property unless he sues you and obtains a court judgment for the amount of the deficiency judgment.

Discharge - The legal term for the elimination of debt through bankruptcy.

Dismissal - The dismissal of bankruptcy case, for all intents and purposes, returns the debtor to the same place it was before bankruptcy was filed.

Dividend - The payment designated by a company's board of directors to be distributed among the holders of outstanding shares of stock.

Examiner - An officer of the court who is appointed to investigate the financial affairs of the debtor.

Equity - In real estate, equity is the difference between the present balance owed on a piece of property and its present market value.

Equity Investment - An investment in the securities or growth category.

Exemption or Exempt Property -Property of an individual debtor that the law protects from the actions of creditors, such as the debtor's residence or homestead, automobile, etc.

Financial Planner - This individual offers financial planning services. A professional financial planner is usually a Certified Financial Planner, a Chartered Financial Consultant, or a Certified Public Accountant.

Foreclosure - The right of a mortgage lender or other creditor with a lien on your house, such as the IRS or a construction mechanics' lien you didn't pay, to force the sale of your house in order to recover what you owe.

Garnishment - Satisfaction of a debt out of the property or wages of the debtor.

General, Unsecured Claim - A claim that is neither secured nor granted a priority by the Bankruptcy Code. Most trade debts are general, unsecured claims.

Guarantor - A person who pledges to repay a loan

or debt in the event the primary debtor does not pay. Many people use guarantors to qualify for a loan or credit card. By using a guarantor (and making regular payments), the primary debtor can improve her credit rating.

Inflow - Cash flow of money coming in on a monthly or annual basis.

Installment Contract - A written agreement to pay for goods or services purchased, in payments of principal and interest, at regularly scheduled intervals.

Interest -The payment that a borrower makes to a lender for the use of money.

Investment - An asset that may increase or decrease in value. Investments include stocks, bonds, real estate, commodities, etc.

Involuntary Bankruptcy Proceeding - In an involuntary bankruptcy proceeding, the debtor is forced into bankruptcy by creditors. Involuntary bankruptcies are relatively rare.

Judgment - The decision issued by a court at the end of a lawsuit. If you are sued and either don't file papers in response within the time allowed, or file papers but eventually lose the case, the plaintiff (the person who sued you) will get a judgment. To attach your wages or put a lien on your property, most creditors need a court judgment.

Judicial Lien - A lien created by the order of a court, such as the lien created by taking a judgment against a debtor.

Leverage - The use of borrowed money with invested funds to increase returns.

Levy and Execution - This is a judicial debt collection procedure in which the court orders the sheriff to seize the debtor's property found in the county to sell in satisfaction of the debtor's debt or debts.

Liability - What a company or individual owes, including debts, loans, mortgages, and other obligation.

Lien - A notice a creditor attaches to your property that (tells the world) that the creditor claims you owe him money. If a creditor puts a lien on your property, you won't be able to sell it without paying off the creditor. A lien makes the property's title or ownership history unclear or cloudy. Without clear title the property can not be sold.

Loan-To-Value Ratio - This is the ratio of the amount borrowed to the value of the property.

Money Market Account - This is a savings account at a bank or savings and loan that pays current interest on the money in the account.

Money Market Fund - A mutual fund that invests only in highly liquid securities.

Necessities - Articles needed to sustain life, such as food, clothing, medical care and shelter.

Non-Exempt Property - The items of property you are not allowed to keep if a creditor gets a judgment against you, puts a lien on your property, or you file for bankruptcy.

Open-Ended Account - One which has no fixed date by which you must pay off the balance, though often a minimum payment is required each month. Credit cards, department store and gasoline accounts are all examples of open-ended accounts.

Outflow - Cash flow of money going out on a monthly or annual basis.

Personal Property - Property that is not permanently attached to land or is moveable.

Petition for Relief - The papers filed initiating a bankruptcy case are called a petition for relief.

Point - An up-front fee charged by a lender. A point equals one percent of the total loan amount.

Post-Judgment Interest - Interest on a court judgment that a creditor may add from the time the judgment is entered in the court clerk's record until you pay it off.

Preference - A transfer of property of the debtor to a creditor made immediately prior to the debtor's bankruptcy that enables the creditor to receive more than they would have received from the bankruptcy. A preferential transfer must be made while the debtor was insolvent and as payment for a debt that existed prior to the transfer of property.

Pre-Judgment Attachment - A legal procedure which lets an unsecured creditor tie up property before obtaining a court judgment. The attachment freezes the property - you can't sell it, spend it (in the case of money), or give it away. If the creditor wins the lawsuit, the property covered by the attachment can be used to pay him.

Pre-Judgment Interest - The interest a creditor is entitled to collect before obtaining a court judgment, under a loan agreement or contract.

Prepayment Penalty - A fee imposed by some lenders in the event you pay off a loan early and the lender doesn't earn all the interest the lender anticipated earning. The penalty is usually a percentage of the balance paid off early.

Prime Rate - The interest rate banks charge their most creditworthy customers.

Principal - The amount owed, minus interest.

Priority - Certain categories of claims are designated as priority claims by the Bankruptcy Code, such as claims for lost wages or taxes. Each classification of claims must be paid in order or priority (the